E-Finance

Andrew Fight

FINANCE

05.03

- Fast track route to mastering the trends and technologies that underpin the development and expansion of e-finance

- Covers the key areas of IT and Internet technologies, as well as competitive trends in the world of banking and the development of existing as well as new banking products that Internet technologies have encouraged

- Examples and lessons from some of the world's most successful businesses, including SWIFT (Society for Worldwide Interbank Financial Telecommunications), the GSTPA (Global Straight Through Processing Association), BOLERO (Bills of Lading Electronic Registry Organisation), as well as ideas from the most innovative companies, including Citicorp, State Street and Charles Schwab

- Includes a glossary of key concepts and a comprehensive resources guide

>>EXPRESS EXEC.COM<<

essential management thinking at your fingertips

First published 2002 by
Capstone Publishing (a Wiley company)
8 Newtec Place
Magdalen Road
Oxford OX4 1RE
United Kingdom
http://www.capstoneideas.com

CIP catalogue records for this book are available from the British Library and the US Library of Congress

ISBN 1-84112-331-5

Printed and bound by CPI Antony Rowe, Eastbourne

Contents

Contents

Introduction to

ExpressExec

ExpressExec is 3 million words of the latest management thinking compiled into 10 modules. Each module contains 10 individual titles forming a comprehensive resource of current business practice written by leading practitioners in their field. From brand management to balanced scorecard, ExpressExec enables you to grasp the key concepts behind each subject and implement the theory immediately. Each of the 100 titles is available in print and electronic formats.

Through the ExpressExec.com Website you will discover that you can access the complete resource in a number of ways:

» printed books or e-books;
» e-content – PDF or XML (for licensed syndication) adding value to an intranet or Internet site;
» a corporate e-learning/knowledge management solution providing a cost-effective platform for developing skills and sharing knowledge within an organization;
» bespoke delivery – tailored solutions to solve your need.

Why not visit www.expressexec.com and register for free key management briefings, a monthly newsletter and interactive skills checklists. Share your ideas about ExpressExec and your thoughts about business today.

Please contact elound@wiley-capstone.co.uk for more information.

Introduction to E-Finance

This chapter sets out the scope of the topic, including:

» what e-finance is;
» the rise of e-finance;
» some technical issues; and
» the transformation of traditional business issues.

"I think there is a world market for maybe five computers."
IBM chairman Thomas Watson, 1943

'There is no reason anyone would want a computer in their home."
DEC chairman Ken Olson, 1977

"640K ought to be enough for anybody."
Microsoft chairman Bill Gates, 1981

This work takes a look at the subject of e-finance, a nascent and heterogeneous field that is tying together hitherto disparate elements into a fully integrated and vast worldwide whole. It is important to understand that change is constant, and technical evolution brings forth its own paradigms for changes that are difficult to foresee. Even industry leaders and visionaries as we see in the above quotes often fail to see the full impact of their nascent technologies. E-finance is developing in ways that are radically transforming not only the business models with which we are familiar but also the world we live in. Where this will lead us in the next 25 years is difficult to say, but one thing is sure – that world will make the present look technologically primitive. We are on the cusp of a new, fully integrated e-finance wired world whose future paradigms have yet to be understood.

This work, then, takes a *"tour d'horizon"* at the world of e-finance, attempting to give it a definition and then covering the historical developments of networks that are coalescing into the world of e-finance. Historical initiatives such as SWIFT, CRM, CLS, electronic funds transfers and online/day trading are looked at, as well as how they interact.

We then look at the evolution of e-finance and understand the origins of this field on the Internet and how this is impacting existing business models, legacy system issues, how new plays or pure plays are circumventing traditional entry barriers, and some of the implementation challenges facing the new and existing players.

Next we consider the global dimension, and understand how various industry initiatives at the global level are impacting economic models in individual countries. From investment banking and corporate banking to initiatives such as BOLERO, GSTPA, global custody, corporate and retail banking and online trading and electronic cash: these are all factors that are discrete sectors, yet which collectively comprise the world of e-finance.

Lastly, we consider some of the key concepts and thinking which will underlie future developments, and draw a series of 10 steps or rules which are necessary success factors to make the e-finance model work not only at the general level but also at the company-specific level.

SOME TECHNICAL ISSUES

The use of information technology (IT) systems in the financial community, from multi-million dollar FX transactions to an individual's cash withdrawal from an automatic teller machine (ATM), touches on every aspect of its day-to-day business. The fact that some institutions spend millions of pounds on IT systems that provide key market information and process transactions a few seconds quicker than a rival institution indicates how much IT impacts banking competitiveness and profitability.

The decision to adopt a particular system or enter into a new market sector is not taken lightly. Apart from front end considerations of trading and quick data analysis are those requiring integration of such systems into the institution's back office, existing legacy systems, and overall IT strategy. Systems also need to be flexible enough to accommodate new products such as derivatives and exploit the briefest of market windows. They need to track markets 24 hours a day, digest global market information, process transactions, and update databases on a real-time basis, with one time data capture and subsequent elimination of human input in the transaction processing. The systems should enable users and management to extract data according to various criteria for use as decisional aid tools. There are several knock-on benefits for the whole organization arising from automating activities:

» Competitiveness is increased as institutions avail themselves of more performing-oriented and rapid systems.
» Customer loyalty is enhanced as a wide range of services is provided and the accuracy and promptness of the service improved.
» Relational databases ensure the consistency of data between offices and enable improved management information systems.

Each bank or e-financial institution has its own specific requirements, and a key to selecting IT systems is determining how those requirements will evolve during the next two to five years. The end-users' input into what information they need, how it should be displayed, and the data capture process are vital to the selection and implementation of such a system. Obtaining input from end-users is therefore crucial to formulating a successful IT strategy. New IT systems also have to be selected so that they integrate themselves seamlessly and transparently into existing IT infrastructures (legacy systems). They should enable existing systems to evolve to satisfy future needs.

Selection criteria depend upon the institution's existing IT systems and strategy. Paramount is the need to secure a tangible return on investment. The selection of a new system or enhancements to existing systems also needs consideration of the telecommunications links between international office networks as well as specific needs.

Risk management is also central to IT strategy. Global derivatives trading and program trading need to be carefully monitored and used within an established risk management framework with appropriate safeguards, authorization levels, and limits control. Good customer relationship management (CRM) systems should enable a better overview of total exposure as well as breakdowns by client, product, or other criteria (interest, currency, credit, etc.). Such systems however are next to useless without appropriate management, regulatory, and security safeguards behind them.

IT systems don't just facilitate but help define the role of front and back offices, whether the user is building on existing systems or implementing a new one. In the latter instance, re-engineering can become a major upheaval as a drive is made towards linking disparate functions across broad product lines. The ultimate aim is invariably to relieve cost pressures defining or redefining the institutions' trading scope.

The amounts to be invested in IT and e-finance systems in the financial services industry over the coming decade are truly awesome. The breadth of such spending, from upgrades, new systems, migrations, value-added services, security, data links, and telecommunications and e-finance will be in the hundreds of millions, indeed billions of dollars. It is virtually impossible to quantify the total anticipated spend over the next few years. One thing is certain – the competitive pressures of the financial marketplace will without any doubt stimulate the demand for state-of-the-art IT systems and value-added integration skills. However, there are essential criteria and methodologies relating to the selection and implementation of advanced systems which remain standard and should be considered by those seeking to implement fundamental change or review of existing IT and business policy.

The aim of this work, therefore, is to address some of these fundamental issues and advanced thinking that lie behind e-finance and IT, whether in a start-up or a re-engineering situation.

WHAT IS E-FINANCE?

The role of IT in finance is vast, and the answer to this question can vary depending upon who the respondent is and in which area of the financial services industry he or she works.

To take a few examples: e-finance can range from the IT systems governing the complex operations of a bank, or specialized subsets of the activity such as secure chip cards; purchases over the Internet; software enabling the compilation of MIS dashboard reports; or use of the Internet to obtain information, diffuse information, or for research purposes. The field broadens when we consider the various electronic networks ranging from ATMs to SWIFT for funds transfer, BOLERO for trade finance, and the new areas of Websites for e-commerce, day trading, and e-finance. The term e-finance basically includes all these facilities, and in this work we will be looking at some of the technological developments in these areas.

Buzzwords circulating in the specialized press include terms such as electronic commerce, digital money, online trading, Web banking, straight through processing, customer relationship management, security, encryption, electronic purse, DHTML, relational databases, etc. These new terms represent the basic elements of 21st century business that are going to revolutionize the way we conduct our business and lead our lives, and in this work we will become familiar with them.

The subject is vast and interrelated, but if we concentrate on e-finance we will see that it focuses on all that relates to the sale of goods and services over electronic networks, and the processing of orders and payments over those networks. These new channels represent the "dematerialization" of traditional modes of distribution in favor of electronic (i.e. "intangible") networks. Despite the nascent state of technological developments to date, this step up the evolutionary ladder promises to be nothing less than revolutionary.

Electronic banking, trading, and finance – these technological developments have a direct impact on the area of business known as electronic commerce (or e-commerce). E-commerce is being made possible due to a unique blend of the following three elements:

» Technology is enabling business to accelerate the transaction cycle by dematerializing it and to do so in a more secure manner.
» Creativity is enabling entrepreneurs to find new ways and methods of doing business outside of traditional structures and methods.
» New methods of raising capital have enabled these innovative businesses to avail themselves of finance.

These three elements, coupled with the trend towards deregulation of the financial markets, mean that the global economic and financial landscape and the financial services industry are going through changes that will affect all players: providers, users, regulators, investors, and consumers. The advent of e-finance means that new patterns of manufacturing, distribution, and consumption will come into effect. E-finance also means that careful consideration will need to be given towards formulating corporate strategies and defining/purchasing the electronic infrastructures necessary to become a successful player.

The development and expansion of communication networks using computers and PCs and their impact on contemporary business models bear comparison to the Industrial Revolution, and the impact of steam and rail power on the traditional agricultural and non-mechanical landscape which then characterized the world.

RISE OF E-FINANCE

Since the advent of the IBM PC in 1981, the past 20 years have already seen prodigious progress. In the pre-PC era, with distribution of information via paper or TV, to e-mail in 1971, the World Wide Web in 1991, the introduction of graphical interfaces (browsers) to access the Web in 1993, and the introduction of online services such as Compuserve in 1995, the Internet (and associated private networks, intranets and extranets) has revolutionized the way millions of people lead their personal and professional lives, and united them in unforeseen ways.

The ability to communicate irrespective of geographic distance, the ability to find and transmit information, the ability to harness this ability to obtain, process, and transmit information instantaneously throughout the world has offered the possibility to transform radically the speed of deal placing. Moreover, the acceleration of information transfer and the simultaneous steady decline in the price of information access and transmission renders the Internet an irresistible attraction to new entrants, and is central to its success. Those players ignoring the new technology do so at their own peril.

To put the pace of technological development available for e-finance in perspective, industry sources (Gartner Group, IDC, Forrester) estimate that the price of computer processing power has fallen by an average of 35% per year over the past three decades, while the cost of sending information over copper, coaxial, fiber, or wireless networks has fallen exponentially. Likewise, the cost of transmitting information has plummeted: it is estimated that the cost of sending 1 trillion bits of information over the network has declined from $150,000 in 1970 to only $0.12 in 2000. A 150-page report can today be e-mailed anywhere on the planet instantaneously for less than the cost of a postage stamp. Ultimately, the Internet serves to reduce the distance between any two PCs on the planet to that of the computer on the desk next to yours. Moreover, the speed of take-up of the PC and the Internet has been far more rapid (years as opposed to decades) than the take-up time required for radio and television.

As the PC and the Internet become increasingly intertwined with daily informational and financial needs, this is expected to further stimulate expansion of the Internet, as evidenced in Table 1.1 (compiled from industry sources).

As a result of these trends, Internet growth and activity is set to expand further over the coming years. With such impressive growth and penetration rates – in such a short period of time – and with substantial anticipated future demand, it is hardly surprising that many businesses, including those in the financial services industry, are looking to the Internet as *the* new medium to deliver products and services.

Table 1.1 PC/Internet growth figures (millions of PCs/people online).

	1995	2000	2005
Computers	237	428	800
Europe			260
USA			230
Asia			190
Latin America			56
Mid East/Africa			30
Other			34
Internet	39	350	750
USA		140	230
Europe			260
Asia			190
Other			70

The growing reach and influence of the Internet, fuelled by cheaper and more powerful PCs and faster and more robust communication links, have helped spawn new ways of doing business. This take-up of computer and Internet technology means that in order to create new business platforms, technology needs to be harnessed by businesses and entrepreneurs who are able to think creatively, and harness this new technology to the design and application of business methods.

TRANSFORMATION OF TRADITIONAL BUSINESS MODELS

Prior to the rise of the PC and the Internet during the 1990s, business models were generally confined to the standard – linking traditional processes of manufacturing, production, and services to logistics, resource acquisition, design, inventory control, processing, shipping – all of which required a large corporate infrastructure.

With the Internet it has become possible for small as well as large entities to provide small and large customers with electronic access to a broad range of information, goods, and services at a cheaper price and with greater efficiency and transparency. Businesses are therefore able to use the Internet to reach a larger and more geographically diverse set of customers at very little incremental cost. In addition, they have been able to leverage technology to expand their businesses very quickly.

Such are the main characteristics of the nascent field of e-commerce and by logical extension, e-finance. It is worth noting that e-commerce is not strictly about selling goods and services through the Web. This view only sees the tip of the iceberg. *E-finance is about using technology fundamentally to change business processes and indeed, build new business processes,* bypassing traditional entry barriers and being able to achieve speed, efficiency, innovation, and customer value. Various industry studies by IDC and Forrester Research note that while in 1996 US e-commerce accounted for some 0. 03% of GDP, by 2002 US e-commerce is expected to account for 7.5–10% of GDP, and to continue to grow even more.

While the USA has been the pacesetter in e-commerce, accounting for 67% of all business-to-business e-commerce revenues and 76% of business-to-consumer e-commerce revenues in 1999, other countries, particularly in Europe and Asia, are increasing their participation and narrowing the gap. Foreign e-commerce will therefore be an important component of global output in the coming years; indeed, IDC predicts that by 2004 62% of e-commerce transactions will come from outside the US, with Western Europe and Japan accounting for the largest shares (35% and 16% of the total, respectively).

The new economy and its successful e-commerce firms are characterized by implementation of new decentralized IT technology, real-time execution and fulfillment, networks of alliances and partnerships with other new economy partners, distributed work processes, and personalized, interactive CRM systems. This new model not only threatens existing processes but is in constant evolution as it shifts from a nascent technology to the new future mainstream economy.

E-commerce and e-finance are breaking established patterns of doing business and defining the "new economy." To traditional companies, this is a threat as they are being forced to adapt to new circumstances and restructure business processes long considered as the "sacred cows." To new entrants, it offers the promise of circumventing hitherto insurmountable entry barriers.

Some Definitions

A quick definition of e-finance, together with:

» CRM;
» STP/CLS;
» SWIFT;
» electronic funds transfer;
» online banking;
» day trading; and
» smart cards.

A QUICK DEFINITION OF E-FINANCE

E-finance can be defined as:

> "All which relates to the linking of business, finance, and banking via electronic means, encompassing information gathering, processing, retrieval, and transmission of data as well as the transmission, purchase, and selling of goods and services."

But the definition broadens when we look at the new possibilities offered by technology. Computers and the use of one time data entry and relational databases means that online real-time data about a company's business and accounts can be generated, enabling managers to manage their companies in new and more proactive ways. A case in point is the use of customer relationship management (CRM) techniques arising from the use of client-driven (as opposed to accounting-driven) relational databases. CRM can assist in providing a more bespoke and personalized service to clients, which in turn impacts on issues of marketing strategy and branding of products and services.

A prime example of this is the online bookstore Amazon.com. Technology at the service of a traditional industry has revolutionized the hitherto staid book industry and enabled the creation of the Amazon "brand" which is merely the fruit of IT and relational databases with savvy marketing.

The field of e-finance however is broader when we consider other factors such as the use of encryption and security at the service of "digital finance" – a broad term we define to include any type of electronic financial service or product. While digital finance has been in existence for many years, and certainly predates the commercial version of the Internet, (e.g. the international bank's payment network SWIFT), the use of new technologies and encryption is enabling a wider propagation of the concept. The phenomenon of "e-finance," like "new economy," "e-commerce" or "e-business," is at present in a nascent state, only hinting at the future networks and services that will be on offer.

One of the first obstacles in considering e-finance is a definition dilemma and, consequently, the lack of an explicit definition of what it encompasses.

The current surge of globalization in the financial sector, considered to be an irreversible and universal trend, has been sparked off by a combination of factors led by the Americanization of the world system. Globalization and internationalization are accompanied by new opportunities and challenges, as well as costs, risks, and threats.

The process of e-finance is not a panacea in itself: it is necessary for development and growth, but it is not enough. From the perspective of developing or transition economies, the "new economy" – e-commerce, e-business, e-finance, etc. – could pose a "deadly threat" which might make these countries secondary or even marginal. However, under certain circumstances, the above-mentioned phenomena may also stand for extraordinary opportunities and the Internet may become the engine of economic growth and development.

The subject is vast but can be divided into several areas that we cover under the following headings:

» CRM
» STP/CLS
» SWIFT
» Electronic funds transfer
» Online banking
» Day trading
» Smart cards.

CRM

The new economy is characterized by companies that have learned how to integrate all of their channels – including the Internet – into one seamless and powerful source for marketing to, selling to, supporting, and servicing customers. These entities are blending technology and strategy in new ways to anticipate customer needs, fulfill demands, build market share, and increase profits. In other words, they are developing *customer relationship management* systems. What exactly is CRM?

CRM is the seamless coordination between sales, customer service, marketing, field support, and other customer-touching functions. Simply put, CRM integrates people, process and technology to maximize relationships with customers and partners, e-customers, traditional customers, distribution channel members, internal customers, and suppliers. What comprises the critical areas of CRM? Some of them are defined as follows:

» *Strategic masterplan*: developing a clear and decisive plan to address the complex people, process, and technology issues of CRM.
» *CRM-enabling technologies*: developing best practices for designing flexible infrastructures and leveraging existing technologies.
» *Integrated marketing applications*: harnessing the latest technologies, Internet solutions and integrated marketing strategies in order to market more effectively.
» *Customer-centric e-business platform*: designing and implementing a customer-facing solution that is integrated with traditional channels by attending this how-to, step-by-step program.
» *Customer contact center (CCC) customer-centric business strategy*: integrating customer contact center technology with existing CRM initiatives.
» *Contact center technology*: communicating with your customers via their preferred channel (Web-based communication, e-mail, interactive voice response, phone, and fax).
» *Mobile and wireless technologies*: identifying those technologies holding the greatest promise for CRM, understanding how they fit together, and implementing them.
» *Winning mobile strategies*: setting goals and developing strategies for deploying wireless solutions with minimum cost and maximum payoff.
» *Data warehousing*: building a better data warehouse to enable leveraging your data for improved strategic decision-making.

CRM enables the automatic capture, route, and qualification of leads by helping the company:

» to understand which marketing programs perform the best;
» to measure the effectiveness of lead generation activities with detailed reporting and analysis;
» to increase awareness, communication, and productivity with a shared, global view of all relevant customer information, with an instant snapshot of company performance; and
» to track automatically the sales pipeline and opportunities, and easily generate forecasts on demand.

Executives can track forecasts at any organizational level including individual representatives, and view monthly breakout of deals and performances sorted to various criteria.

STP/CLS

Straight through processing and/or *continuous linked settlement* are other areas of e-finance that are revolutionizing the traditional ways in which banks conduct their business. Reshaping global FX (foreign exchange) trading cycles is becoming an area of key interest as technology rises to become available. See Chapter 7, also Chapter 9 for Website link.

STP – straight through processing

STP is a concept being championed by the Global Straight Through Processing Association (GSTPA), an organization set up by key players in the industry (see Chapter 7). STP relates to the concept of one time deal capture as depicted in Fig. 2.1.

The basic idea is that the transaction data are entered once upon deal capture and that all subsequent transaction processes are effected using the data keyed in at source, and the data flows through all the required steps of the electronic trade processing procedure. The reduction in data capture and automated processing aims to accelerate the settlement cycle, reduce the possibility of error and settlement risk, and enable the extraction of data for management information reporting purposes.

CLS – continuous linked settlement

CLS is closely related to STP. It was founded with the object of eliminating settlement risk, which is inherent in all foreign exchange transactions using current settlement methods. The Bank of International Settlements, in its report on *Settlement Risk in Foreign Exchange Transactions* of March 1996, defines settlement risk as follows:

"Settlement of a foreign exchange (FX) trade requires the payment of one currency and the receipt of another. In the absence of a settlement arrangement that ensures that the final transfer of one

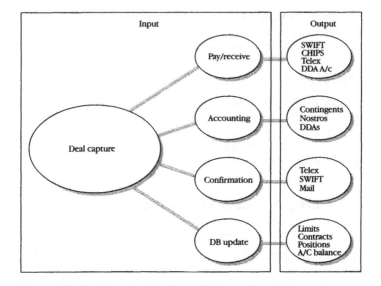

Fig. 2.1 One time transaction input.

currency will occur if and only if the final transfer of the other currency also occurs, one party to an FX trade could pay out the currency it sold but not receive the currency it bought. This principal risk in the settlement of foreign exchange transactions is variously called foreign exchange settlement risk or cross-currency settlement risk."

A risk associated with settlement risk is *liquidity risk*. It can be differentiated into two forms:

» *Market liquidity risk*, which arises when a firm is unable to conclude a large transaction in a particular instrument at anything near the current market price.
» *Funding liquidity risk*, which is defined as the inability to obtain funds to meet cashflow obligations.

The second dimension to settlement risk is the associated *credit risk*. If a transaction cannot be settled, the party having paid out first faces the risk of fully losing the principal amount of the transaction. The party's exposure equals the full amount.

Awareness of settlement risk and its potential effects on global markets was highlighted in 1974, through the failure of Bankhaus Herstatt, a small foreign exchange trading bank in Germany. At that time, some of its counterparties had irrevocably paid DM to the bank during the day but before the banking license was withdrawn. They had done so in good faith, anticipating the receipt of US dollars later in the same day in New York. Herstatt's New York correspondent bank suspended all outgoing US dollar payments from Herstatt's account. The counterparties were therefore fully exposed to the value of traded Deutschmarks.

The term "Herstatt-Risk" was coined to describe this kind of settlement risk. It occurs when one party pays out the currency it sold but does not receive the currency it bought. During the banking day, the bank's banking license was withdrawn and it was ordered into liquidation by the German authorities. This happened after the close of the German interbank payments system.

As trading volumes rose (daily global FX volumes reached US$3trn in the 1990s), central banks became more and more interested and concerned about the potential disruptive consequences on financial markets due to settlement risk.

Establishment of CLS Services

In 1995, a group of major FX trading banks (known as the Group of 20 or G20, with UBS as major participant) got together to consider how the private sector might develop a solution to the problem of settlement risk. The result of this study was the CLS concept. In July 1997, the G20 banks formed a company, CLS Services Ltd (CLSS), to develop and build the CLS system. The initial shareholders of CLSS were the G20 banks. CLS differentiates between "settlement members" and "user members."

Settlement members maintain accounts with CLS Bank in the eligible CLS currencies and can submit trades directly to CLS. Members are responsible for the net funding obligations of all transactions submitted.

User members have no direct accounting relationship with CLS Bank. They are able to submit trades directly to CLS but they have to rely on a settlement member to settle their transactions over CLS.

Both memberships enable direct submission of trades for non-members, which are also known as "third parties." CLS members can carry out settlements on behalf of third parties. These transactions are the direct responsibility of the particular CLS member submitting them.

Impact of CLS

E-finance technology is at the heart of CLS since the data capture and deal flows will all be processed electronically. The main advantage will be reduced settlement risk; but also reduced settlement periods, resulting in increased efficiency in the management of the FX "float" – the period of time prior to clearance when the funds are "in limbo" and not generating a return. Reduction in settlement from three days to one day offers the possibility of substantial revenues due to more proactive management of these deals.

The impact of CLS will be the elimination of settlement risk of foreign exchange deals in the eligible CLS currencies. As a consequence, provisions taken to cover losses through settlement risk can be lowered. Settlement risk still exists for non-CLS banks. It is therefore expected that banks that do not want to invest in CLS, or cannot become CLS members, will look for means and services to have access to CLS and perform foreign exchange transactions settlement risk-free.

As deals are settled across CLS' books and only net positions are relevant, it follows that thousands of deals can be settled with a very limited number of payment orders issued by settlement members. This will lower transaction costs for banks considerably. Indirectly, operational risk is lowered because fewer payments will be generated and therefore fewer errors can occur in processing them. Over time, CLS will be expected to reduce the volume of transactions cleared through the relevant national RTGS (real time gross settlement) system; this will affect the profitability of the "vanilla" currency clearing business and cause banks to expand the range of services offered. Current estimates project a 30% decrease in the number of transactions.

As the technology matures, these new developments will not be confined to the foreign exchange market but could possibly extend to other cash-based products, and must be extended to the securities world in order to support an intra-day securities market.

SWIFT

Background

SWIFT, the Society for Worldwide Interbank Financial Telecommunications, is the worldwide banking telecommunications network founded by international banks in 1973 in direct competition with the telex and private networks. SWIFT's business is to support the financial data communication and processing needs of financial institutions. Its markets are financial institutions conducting business in payments, foreign exchange, money markets, securities trading, and trade finance.

SWIFT provides financial data communications and exchanges that are secure and reliable. With products and services supported by an organization of 1200 professionals based in key financial centers around the world, SWIFT has been at the forefront of automating the financial services industry for years. Customer benefits are:

» replacement of paper-based processing through automated procedures using SWIFT standards; and
» increased productivity, cost reductions, control of financial risk, and exposure through integrated end-to-end transaction processing between financial institutions and their own customers.

SWIFT's head office is located at la Hulpe in Belgium. It has regional offices in:

» New York (Americas)
» Hong Kong and Tokyo (Asia-Pacific)
» Brussels and London (Europe, Middle East, and Africa).

There are branch offices as well as agents in various areas. SWIFT's sales activities are divided into five regions:

» Americas
» Asia/Pacific

» Europe North (including UK, English-speaking Africa, Middle East)
» Europe South West (including French-speaking Africa and the French Overseas Departments & Territories)
» Europe Central & East.

Development

The network originally began operations with the SWIFT I service which was designed in the early 1970s. As transaction volumes grew, the original network was upgraded and new services were added.

SWIFT II was the second generation of network services. The main feature of this system and the SWIFT transport network was the ability to handle the ever-growing volume of users' messages quickly, effectively, and securely. The system was made up of a number of active components (in the form of computers or other intelligent devices) linked together by communications links to form a global network.

» A single system control processor (SCP) monitored and controlled the entire SWIFT II system. It controlled access to the system by validating all requests but did not process financial messages.
» Slice processors (SPs) provided the message switching power of the system (i.e. routing and safe storage of messages). Each SP controlled a number of end-user destination addresses.
» Regional processors (RPs) enabled individual users to connect to the SWIFT II system. Substantial text validation was performed by the RPs, hence reducing the overheads on the SPs.
» Lastly, communications processors (CPs) provided the connections to the transport network required at a particular RP.

SWIFT II was eventually replaced by SWIFTAlliance, a series of terminals operating on UNIX open systems, thereby enabling banks to enjoy hardware independence and not be tied into the proprietary systems conundrum.

About the time that SWIFTAlliance was implemented (early to mid 1990s), the Internet began to exhibit its phenomenal growth. Implementation of the Internet and formation of cross-industry initiatives such as GSTPA (setting up effectively parallel networks threatening the monopoly) led SWIFT to take a more extroverted look at industry developments. The result was SWIFT leveraging on its skills set of providing secure financial payment, messaging systems, and international networks to enter the arena of the Internet, and to offer credible services and a larger range of facilities to its clientele.

Future developments

SWIFT, as the world's premier financial telecommunications service provider, is not immune to the trends and restructurings occurring in the banking and IT fields. Recent initiatives by the consortium aim to extend its presence into the Internet via payments and financial messaging. SWIFTNet is an effort to develop a secure network that can be used for CLS or any other market infrastructure, thereby enlarging the scope of SWIFT offerings.

» Release 1 of SWIFTNet was delivered in March 2000 and met all the deliverables for CLS, one of the first early adopter market infrastructures. It included the deployment of the secure Internet Protocol network (SIPN); an initial version of SWIFTNet InterAct, the interactive messaging service; and the SWIFTNet Link and SWIFTNet security software. This first release has already processed more than 11 million messages as part of the ongoing CLS trials.

» Release 2, including an interactive service that can be used for CLS or any other financial market infrastructure, moved into pilot phase in September 2000. This will allow other early adopters such as GSTPA and central banking institutions to begin tailoring their own applications. This second release also includes a range of connectivity options including SWIFTAlliance Webstation and the SWIFTAlliance Gateway interface for application-to-application messaging and connectivity with host platforms.

» Release 3 became operationally live in 2001 and adds SWIFTNet FileAct bulk messaging capability.

SWIFT is betting on the likelihood that SWIFTNet will replace its existing financial messaging service (FIN). It is also hoping that SWIFTNet will offer considerable potential to support the business of SWIFT members well beyond the traditional areas FIN serves today, such as e-commerce, pre-trade, and low value payments. In order to avoid losing clients, SWIFT has developed the following approach to evolve its FIN and SWIFTNet service propositions, and aims to introduce capabilities to SWIFTNet in stages.

» Firstly, the provision of the core FIN store-and-forward messaging service will be preserved for the foreseeable future.
» Secondly, access to FIN and SWIFTNet services through a single window interface and technical platform will be encouraged to reduce costs and support the build-up of a critical mass of endpoints on SWIFTNet.
» Lastly, SWIFT will continue to enhance the SWIFTNet services to respond to new requirements, provide alternatives to FIN when required, and support the implementation of new and re-engineered standards.

FIN is here to stay for a number of years and SWIFT will gradually enhance the value proposition of SWIFTNet. Clients will be able to access FIN through the SWIFTNet environment as the security structure and message standards of FIN will remain unchanged, but members will now simply be accessing it over an IP infrastructure instead of the existing X.25 Communications Protocol infrastructure.

SWIFT is well aware of the potential of the Internet despite current drawbacks – and has begun research into how it can harness its power to extend the SWIFTNet offering. This corroborates the decision to develop an e-commerce strategy for SWIFT. Since the decision was taken, a dedicated e-team has been working closely with the board B2B working group. The group believes that it is in a powerful position, on behalf of its worldwide community of members, to set the standards for trust and payments in B2B e-commerce, as, according to a spokesman, " it already has the network, messaging infrastructure, standards capability, and market power to achieve this. The role of SWIFT will be to provide an Internet messaging infrastructure for carrying these and other trusted transactions."

The service, called Trust Act, is an Internet-based messaging infrastructure that SWIFT will run on behalf of its members. Buyers and sellers will have Trust Act software loaded on their browser or enterprise system. "Essentially Trust Act is a site on the Internet, maintained in SWIFT's secure operations centers," the spokesman explained. "This joint solution leverages SWIFT's messaging strengths."

SWIFT is also undertaking work in the area of supporting B2B e-payments through an evolving service, called "PrepaymentsPlus." This work covers messaging, standards setting, rulebook development, payment scheme selection and supporting applications. Trust Act will carry the corporate-to-bank messaging as a payload over the Internet. Bank-to-bank messaging will still use SWIFTNet. The group therefore aims to leverage its legacy offerings and expertise in standards setting and rulebook development, to position the consortium in new areas and design corporate-to-bank payments standards.

See Chapter 9 for Website link.

ELECTRONIC FUND TRANSFER

Electronic fund transfers, automatic teller machines, debit and smart cards, point-of-sale mechanisms, home PC banking/trading services, and digital securities transfers have been a part of the financial landscape for decades. For instance, consumers and businesses have been accustomed to transferring funds digitally, rather than physically, for many years, debiting and crediting accounts via computers rather than physically withdrawing and redepositing currency. The electronic fund transfer (EFT) – a mechanism used to send "digital money" across the wire from one account to another – has been in widespread use for decades and forms the core of electronic payments between companies, governments, and other institutions. More than $5trn in electronic payments occurs every day – including $2trn that is transferred between banks; large-value electronic payment systems and clearing houses such as SWIFT, CHIPS, ACH, CHAPS, BACS, and others are a fundamental component of the electronic payment network.

Other electronic mechanisms for obtaining cash, moving funds, and completing purchases have been in use for years and are well entrenched in today's society. Consumers have actively used automatic teller machines (ATMs) since the 1980s, accessing cash, depositing funds, and transferring balances with their ATM cards. Though ATMs took more than 15 years to become firmly established in consumer banking, they are now an indispensable part of retail finance: ATMs currently account for 50% of all cash-based banking transactions and have replaced many of the functions previously handled by branch-based tellers.

ONLINE BANKING

The history of phone banking and PC dial-up services dates back some 20 years. Through basic technology, customers have been able to manage funds and payments using phone keypads and computers. This variant of e-finance, however, is primitive compared with the future promises of this technology, which will enable a far more proactive involvement and richer functionality to the end-user than has hitherto been possible.

PC-based online banking started in the late 1970s and early 1980s with proprietary dial-up services. Banks such as Chemical and Citibank offered, for a monthly fee, a basic home-based PC banking service which included balance look-up, fund transfers, and bill payment. The efforts to promote these services, however, never really took off due to high user fees and cumbersome interfaces which were further handicapped by slow response times, complicated access procedures, and uncertain security.

In the mid 1980s software companies such as Intuit introduced third-party software solutions (Quicken) to act as an interface, linking customers and banks. Customers could use the platform to access account information, transfer funds and pay bills. Customers could also authorize the payment of funds to a given merchant. Quicken would then process the customer approval and determine (via Intuit Services Corporation (ISC)) if the merchant was part of the Federal Reserve's Automated Clearing House (ACH). If so, ISC would effect an electronic payment through the ACH and, if not, would mail a check to the merchant.

DAY TRADING

Securities transactions including stock and bond trading have also been driven by technology for the past few decades. While it has been common for many years to pass stock/bond orders through brokers, who then transmit verbal or electronic information to an exchange and then revert with appropriate debits and credits to cash and securities accounts, actual physical possession of the securities is practically non-existent. Instead, many securities now exist only in a "dematerialized" electronic form and are transferred between seller and buyer by computer.

Discount brokerage companies, such as Schwab, started offering basic PC trading capabilities via proprietary software accessing services via a dial-up connection with an ISP (AOL, Compuserve) in the mid-to-late 1980s. The increasing complexity of software and the need for augmented data feeds now means that ideally an ISDN connection is needed to engage in online day trading.

Day trading is the buying and selling of stock in such a way that at the end of each day you have no holdings. In other words, you "close your position" and sell whatever securities you bought before the close of the day. This is the pure definition and may not always be either possible or feasible. There may be times when you may either accidentally or on purpose find yourself holding overnight. If you do this more often than not you then become a "short time trader" and if you hold even longer, you become an "investor."

The uniqueness of day trading is that you are simply playing against other day traders and could not care less about the company, what brokers think about the stock, or even what the company does. The day trader is merely concerned with the movement of the stock during the day and profiting from it. What do you need to be a day trader?

» A brokerage account. There are numerous e-brokerage accounts. Many of these Websites can be accessed over the Internet.

» Computer with Web access. Some may say this is not needed and they would technically be right, but it is very hard to play this game without one. Day trading relies on speed: speed of getting information and speed on reacting to information, and a computer just makes it faster. The facilities you will be accessing include:

  » news, stock quotes, charts etc.; and
  » your broker – you can get in and out of stocks quicker online than you can by phone.

» Proprietary software. Many of the e-brokerages will provide you with specialized software to be able to execute the trades directly on your PC screen. Some e-brokerages even provide specialized training services to familiarize novices with the mechanics of day trading and the features of the software. Some software may require special graphics cards in the PC in order to have a two-monitor display that can contain the several user screens required for the trading activity.

SMART CARDS

Smart cards and stored value cards (monetary and token-based), embedded with integrated circuits (ICs) and capable of holding identities, authorizations, certificates, records, and monetary value are another significant feature of e-finance. They were originally invented by Roland Moreno in France, and were developed by Bull Computers in France. Developed in the late 1960s they began to appear in "workable" form in the late 1970s. They have gradually increased in popularity since that time – particularly in Europe, where more than 100 million were in circulation at the end of the 1990s. Their use ranges from simple phone cards to credit cards, and now even cards to access medical services, embedded with key data about the cardholder. Another example – smart cards can be used for pay-TV subscriptions.

The smart card is one of the developments from the world of information technology that will have a significant impact on e-finance. Similar in size to today's plastic credit card, the smart card has a microprocessor or memory chip embedded in it. The chip stores electronic data and programs that are protected by advanced security features. When coupled with a reader, the smart card has the processing power to serve many different applications such as secure transactions over electronic networks (e.g. SWIFT). Smart cards can also act as an access-control device, to ensure that personal and business data, or indeed secure offices or facilities, are available only to authorized users.

Smart cards can also store "digital cash" or "electronic money" to enable users to effect purchases or exchange value over electronic networks. Providing data portability, security, and convenience, smart cards come in two varieties: memory cards and microprocessor cards. Memory cards simply store data and can be viewed as a data storage device with optional security, while microprocessor cards can add, delete, and manipulate information in its memory on the card. There are different types of security mechanisms – those necessary for a memory-only card are less sophisticated than those for a microprocessor card. Access to the information contained in a smart card is controlled two ways:

» who can access the information (everybody, the cardholder or a specific third party); and

» how the information can be accessed (read only, added to, modified or erased).

One form of protection is ciphering, which is like translating the information into some unknown foreign language. Some smart cards are capable of ciphering and deciphering (translating back to an easily understood form) so the stored information can be transmitted without compromising confidentiality. The important thing about smart cards is that they are everyday objects that people can carry in their pockets, yet they have the capacity to retain and protect critical information stored in electronic form. The proliferation of this technology is evident when one considers that the same electronic function can be performed by embedding similar circuits in other everyday objects, such as key rings, watches, glasses, rings, and earrings.

Contactless card technology also offers significant potential in that it can enable the manipulation of "tags." Tags function like contactless smart cards but are in the form of a ring, sticker, or baggage label. They can be attached to objects such as gas bottles, cars or animals, and can hold and protect information concerning that object. This allows the object to be managed by an information system or customer relationship management system without any manual data handling. The possibilities of such systems in areas such as inventory control and trade finance are limitless.

The current state of development of smart cards is relatively new, and has already made a significant impact in increasing the security of transactions and dramatically limiting the incidence of fraudulent transactions. For example, in France, which has adopted the smart card as the standard payment mechanism of choice for credit cards, the rate of fraudulent use plummeted from several percent (3–5% unofficially) to under 0.5%, radically reducing the cost of fraud to banks. Other countries such as the US and the UK have yet to adopt this French-developed technology, no doubt for reasons of national preference. The smart card is in its infancy and it promises ultimately to influence the way business, data processing, and e-finance are conducted.

Evolution of E-Finance

The origin and rise of e-finance and Internet commerce, plus a timeline.

ORIGIN OF E-FINANCE AND INTERNET COMMERCE

E-finance, as we have seen in the previous chapter, began with the development of several disparate elements, many of which were developed in isolation. As these individual elements progressed, they began to be tied together in networks. The true era of *Internet-enabled* e-finance began in the mid 1990s when the Internet became the network of networks. This enabled businesses and banks to communicate in hitherto unforeseen ways, in transmitting information and payments, but also in conducting business.

Businesses then began to develop Web-based platforms to deliver financial services. The process started in the B2C sector and has gradually moved into the B2B arena as systems became more robust and secure. As different groups began developing business models for the banking industry, several clear advantages have become evident.

» Using the Internet, companies can use standard Internet communications protocols (TCP/IP) and meta-languages (XML extensible markup language) and OFX (open financial exchange) to conduct electronic business flexibly and dynamically.

» E-finance platforms enable Internet payments systems to be linked together and to process customer payments more efficiently, while technology enables the creation of user-friendly GUIs (graphical user interfaces), which help promote interest and activity among consumers.

» Smart cards promise to add additional security to the development of electronic purchases and transactions.

» Increased volume usage, moreover, leads to a lowering of unit transaction costs and the development of secure payment mechanisms such as firewalls, encryption, and digital signatures.

Not surprisingly, it was the smaller players and institutions which adopted these technologies, seeing them as a means of bypassing traditional costly entry barriers to the business, rather than the large Wall Street institutions which were quite content to operate in the *status quo* and protect their turf. Such pioneers include companies like Charles Schwab, the online broker, and Ameritrade. Other smaller players also began as start-ups, obtaining capital from venture capitalists or incubator funds. While many companies have since evolved into broader and more sophisticated platforms, all of them began life as corporate storefronts, promoting proprietary products and services through their own company-specific Websites.

RISE OF E-FINANCE AND ELECTRONIC TRADING

Discount broker Schwab began providing its customers with a rudimentary PC trading access in 1984. The service was basic and cumbersome and routed through relatively slow dial-up access. True online trading began in the USA in 1995 when the first initial public offering (IPO) of a company was placed via the Internet. Over 3500 investors purchased shares, marking this the first time securities had actually been sold via the Web.

The Securities & Exchange Commission (SEC) was concerned about this new activity and the potential precedent it might establish; it therefore investigated the initial offering and the ongoing secondary trading. The SEC subsequently issued a "no-action letter" sanctioning the transaction, effectively giving the green light to true Internet-based trading. This led to other players beginning trading. Here are some of these.

» Web Street Securities, E*Trade, Schwab, Ameritrade, and Datek, who altered their existing discount brokerage operations in the same year and migrated to the Internet.
» Web Street Securities, a "pure play" (i.e. one which exists only in a computerized state with no traditional "bricks and mortar" offices or infrastructure), commenced its operations in 1996 by offering customers a full-service information and execution platform.
» Schwab also began operations in 1996 by building its Web-based platform and offering innovative online services and competitive pricing.

Full service brokers, such as Merrill Lynch, Morgan Stanley Dean Witter, and Paine Webber, in contrast, preferred to wait and see the results. By 2000 Schwab had 3.5 million active online accounts (equal to 50% of its total client base) and was executing nearly 250,000 trades per day. Discount brokers, which had already embraced technology such as phone banking and PC banking during the 1980s, took advantage of these crumbling entry barriers and were particularly successful in adapting to the Internet.

Internet banking also came to the fore: the first true Internet bank was Security First Network Bank (SFNB), created in Atlanta in 1995. In that year the Office of Thrift Supervision approved the proposal to change First Federal's business focus from that of a savings institution to a pure play electronic bank. Finance company Cardinal received approval in mid-1995, changed the bank's name to SFNB and commenced operations by offering Web-based balance look-up, unlimited third-party bill paying, funds transfers, loans, and Federal Deposit Insurance Corporation (FDIC) insured deposits.

As is typical in the field of banking information technology, software and e-finance infrastructure systems developed for in-house uses have applications in other industry sectors and can, in turn, be sold to defray development costs and generate profits. Hence, players who have developed Web platforms can in turn forge links combining their proprietary technology solutions with other solutions providers in the IT sphere. Hence, new entities arise which can offer financial institutions an Internet turnkey product for online banking.

With very few exceptions, the world's largest financial institutions have generally failed to act as innovators and movers in Web-based finance, and have delayed their offerings until new innovative start-ups had built considerable market shares and brand identification. The initial lack of interest or foresight of major players meant that many of them found themselves chasing the upstarts during the late 1990s. Once it became clear that Internet-based commerce was a new force that was here to stay, the major players, with deep pockets, began to change their tune and pay attention to the developments and issues being raised by e-commerce and e-finance.

In other words, institutions moved from denying the need to have an Internet presence and using the Internet as a medium to diffuse "brochureware," to employing it as an aggressive, transaction-enabled business-gathering tool. These institutions also realized that the Internet allowed them to create a new "high tech" image, offer new products/services, and enlarge reach/presence without having to spend additional capital on physical expansion. Full service brokers such as Merrill Lynch and Morgan Stanley Dean Witter hence rushed to redefine their business models and provide customers with services that more Internet-aggressive firms such as Schwab and Ameritrade were already supplying.

Merrill Lynch moreover had to back out of the corner it had painted itself into in late 1998 when it declared that "the do-it-yourself model of investing, centered on Internet trading, should be considered as a serious threat to Americans' financial lives." It is particularly ironic that large Wall Street securities firms, which pride themselves on being adept, dynamic, and responsive – as, in fact, they are – were unable to adapt to the new business paradigm with the same agility.

TIMELINE

1985
» Classic electronic proprietary networks.
» SWIFT installs a high volume satellite link between US and European operations.

1986
» Internet Engineering Task Force established.

1988
» First Internet worm virus.

1991
» WWW released by CERN.

1992
» SWIFT introduces Interbank file transfer.
» World bank comes online.
» Term "surfing the Internet" is coined by Jean Armour Polly.

1993
» InterNIC is created by the National Science Foundation (USA) to provide Internet services (domain name).
» UN goes online.
» Mosaic is the first browser.
» Extension of MIME (multipurpose Internet mail extensions).

1994

- » Marc Andreesen, one of the developers of Mosaic, left NCSA, co-founded Netscape Communications Corp., released the Netscape Navigator, a graphical Web browser.
- » House/Senate provide information servers.
- » Shopping malls arrive on the Internet.
- » SWIFT introduces SWIFTAlliance UNIX-based terminals.

1995

- » Microsoft stepped into the Web browser market, released the Internet Explorer version 1.0.
- » Traditional online dial-up systems (Compuserve, America Online, Prodigy) begin to provide Internet access.
- » A number of Net-related companies go public, with Netscape leading the pack with the 3rd largest-ever NASDAQ IPO share value (9 August).
- » Two of the biggest names in e-commerce are launched: Amazon.com and eBay.com.
- » Technologies of the year: WWW, search engines.
- » Emerging technologies: mobile code (JAVA, JAVAscript), virtual environments (VRML), collaborative tools.
- » Hacks of the year: The Spot (12 June), Hackers Movie Page (12 August).

1996

- » SWIFT gears up for STP with a dedicated team.
- » Technologies of the year: search engines, JAVA, Internet phone.
- » Emerging technologies: virtual environments (VRML), collaborative tools, Internet appliance (network computer).
- » Technologies of the year: e-commerce, e-auctions, portals.
- » Emerging technologies: e-trade, XML, intrusion detection.

1997

- » June, 35 million Internet users.
- » CLS Services Ltd established.

1998

- » June, 60 million Internet users.

» Companies flock to the Turkmenistan network Information Center in order to register their name under the .tm domain, the English abbreviation for trademark.

1999

» June, 130 million Internet users.
» First Internet Bank of Indiana, the first full-service bank available only on the Net, opens for business on 22 February.
» First large-scale cyberwar takes place simultaneously with the war in Serbia/Kosovo.
» Retail spending over the Internet reaches $20bn, according to Business.com.
» .ps is registered to Palestine (11 October).
» Emerging technologies: Net-cell phones, thin computing, embedded computing.
» Viruses of the year: Melissa (March), ExploreZip (June).

2000

» A massive denial of service attack is launched against major Websites, including Yahoo, Amazon, and eBay in early February.
» After months of legal proceedings, the French court rules that Yahoo! must block French users from accessing hate memorabilia in its auction site (Nov). Given its inability to provide such a block on the Internet, Yahoo! removes those auctions entirely (January 2001).
» SWIFT announces plans for two services for trust and payments into the business-to-business domain: TrustAct, which assures the identity of corporates trading over the internet and e-paymentsPlus, which provides corporates with web-based payment initiation and assurance services.
» Technologies of the year: ASP, Napster.
» Emerging technologies: wireless devices, IPv6.
» Viruses of the year: Love Letter (May).

2001

» Afghanistan's Taliban bans Internet access countrywide, including from Government offices, in an attempt to control content (13 July).
» Code Red worm and Sircam virus infiltrate thousands of Web servers and e-mail accounts, respectively, causing a spike in Internet bandwidth usage and security breaches (July).

» A fire in a train tunnel running through Baltimore, Maryland seriously damages various fiber-optic cable bundles used by backbone providers, disrupting Internet traffic in the Mid-Atlantic states and creating a ripple effect across the US (18 July).

The E-Dimension

» The legacy system and migration issues;
» entry barriers to e-finance; and
» implementation issues.

LEGACY SYSTEM AND MIGRATION ISSUES

The "pure play" B2C financial services model, which formed part of the first wave of pioneering digital finance platforms, is a concept that is still being tested and developed. Pure plays are not weighted down with legacy systems and therefore have the advantage of being able to design and create new models with a clean slate. There are no migration costs, database conversions, or sacred cows to slay. Established "bricks and mortar" companies in contrast are endowed with existing structures, and must therefore develop their B2C or B2B platforms alongside these models. This situation is known as a "legacy system" as companies are required to develop new models over existing ones that are their "legacy."

Many of the issues relating to legacy systems are graphically depicted in Fig. 4.1.

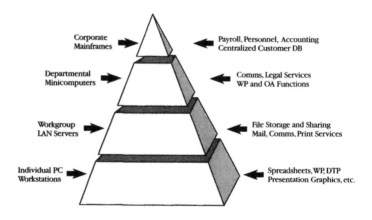

Fig. 4.1 Legacy systems - typical configuration.

Dealing with legacy systems is fraught with complexity because in many cases, less than ideal solutions may need to be developed in order to interface with legacy systems. This can serve to increase development costs and yield somewhat less than satisfactory solutions. Pure plays, on the other hand, are not burdened with these issues and can therefore develop their business models on a clean slate. Once operational, pure plays tend to function more cost-effectively by avoiding not only the legacy systems issue but also the corporate overheads normally associated with "bricks and mortar" operations. However, developing the model is fraught with uncertainty as there are no precedents to build upon. A savvy knowledge of the markets (business knowledge) and an understanding of the capabilities of information technologies (IT knowledge) are indispensable in forming the new e-finance company.

Pure plays can create new models in the areas of online trading, online banking, or a hybrid of the two. The natures of the businesses, however, are different.

» Online trading is a more dynamic and interactive experience than online banking. While it requires customer support, it does not necessarily need to grant customers immediate access to cash.
» Online banks need to be able to accept and deliver cash in some form and must therefore enter the physical realm by forming an alliance with an ATM or bank network, adding to the cost of the model.
» Hybrids must also contend with legacy system integration in order to ensure smooth and accurate communication between established technology and the Web portal. This type of integration can be very expensive, particularly for large financial institutions. For example, Citibank reportedly spent $500mn integrating its legacy data processing with its Web platform.

The constraints arising from legacy system integration lead to certain paradoxes, as summarized in Fig. 4.2.

While the B2C e-finance sector was first to develop business models, and received most of the popular press coverage, the B2B e-finance sector represents a far larger and deeper market due to the scale of business volumes being conducted. Most Internet-related B2B efforts began in the late 1990s, in the wake of the development of the B2C sector. The development of initiatives related to online trading in FX, bonds, commodities, and derivatives, as well as initiatives in other areas such as corporate banking and syndicated lending, are relatively recent phenomena, not least because of perceived security risk issues and large transaction amounts.

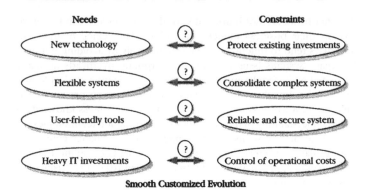

Fig. 4.2 Paradoxes facing banks today.

Despite the late start, B2B e-finance is now a growing source of activity for providers and users. Most global financial institutions are well represented in transaction-enabled B2B ventures through internally developed efforts, alliances, partnerships and/or investments, some of which we will see in Chapter 5, "The Global Dimension." Indeed, the largest players have moved aggressively to participate in a range of ventures by setting up specialized e-subsidiaries, seeking to protect themselves against any future developments or structural changes in the global marketplace.

Of course, certain aspects of the financial markets have traded in electronic form, if not yet in Internet form, for the better part of one to two decades. The best-known example of this is SWIFT, the Society for Worldwide Interbank Financial Telecommunications (Chapter 2). This market, which is dominated by banks, processes some $1.5trn daily. Other entities using electronic networks are the FX markets, as well as certain equity and futures markets. NASDAQ (the National Association of Securities Dealers Automated Quotes) has existed as an electronic market since its creation in 1971 while others, such as the London Stock Exchange (LSE), migrated from physical open-outcry trading forums to electronic trading forums during the 1980s and 1990s. Other European countries such as France have their own electronic payments networks (SAGGITAIRE and RELIT).

Other specialized markets have migrated from physical to electronic trading systems, the best-known in Europe being the London International Financial Futures Exchange (LIFFE), and the Marché à Terme International de France (MATIF).

ENTRY BARRIERS TO E-FINANCE

While e-finance offered new players the ability to circumvent traditional entry barriers to the financial services industry, as it matures it is developing its own set of industry specializations and criteria. E-finance is demolishing traditional entry barriers and business models but it is also creating new ones. The erosion of entry barriers can occur due to a variety of factors – business, technological, and regulatory. Notable changes in the regulatory environment, for example, include:

» "big bang" – the deregulation of the London stock market in 1986 (eliminating fixed commissions and dissolving the distinction between brokers and jobbers [dealers]);
» passage of the Riegle-Neal Act in 1994 (allowing US banks to serve customers across state lines);
» deregulation of the Tokyo stock market in the 1990s (eliminating fixed commissions and allowing the creation of discount brokers);
» erosion of the Glass-Steagall Act in the late 1990s (dividing the banking industry into investment and commercial banks, allowing them to participate in each other's markets); and
» globalization and financial deregulation.

These developments, coupled with technological innovation, have led to a blurring between traditional and e-finance environments. As deregulation continues to make its way around the world and new entrants enter particular areas of the financial services industry, competition in e-finance will accelerate. For better or worse, formidable entry barriers have historically protected the finance industry. New entrants to the financial markets have needed strong management (including networks and contacts), a deep knowledge of legal, operational, transaction, and credit risk, substantial financial resources, efficient customer service, and technological prowess.

As financial services have gravitated to the Internet some of these barriers to entry have already been eroded; however, many of the specific skills relating to the financial services industry need to be honed and developed further. For example, risk management needs to become more robust in the face of increasing speed and volatility in the markets. This need translates into the need for efficient database management, one time data entry at deal capture, and the production of online real time management information systems reports.

Management

A strong management team is a critical requirement for every financial or Internet e-finance venture, and indeed the successful ones need to operate with a combination of bankers and IT staff that can work together. With waves of layoffs in the financial services industry, many seasoned banking and technology professionals have opted to move to start-ups, seeking a chance to participate in an entrepreneurial, rather than traditional corporate, venture (and being tempted, perhaps, by share options in the start-up).

Established institutions are obviously not oblivious to these threats and are therefore seeking to develop their own Internet presence. Hence, major players such as JP Morgan Chase, Merrill Lynch, Deutsche Bank, Dresdner Bank, HSBC, Citibank, Bank of America, *et al* have "seconded" top executives to their new Internet ventures.

Liquidity and risk management

Another matter of concern to start-ups is ensuring that sufficient capital is available to support the entire range of business and operating risks; insufficient capital can still act as an entry barrier and impact liquidity for ongoing operations. Risk can assume various forms: classic credit risk from loans, derivatives risk, interest rate risk, currency rate risk, legal risk, documentation risk, and compliance risk. Sufficient liquidity is therefore essential in ensuring that the company can weather market volatility. Entry barriers can be made more difficult by issues of brand name, image and "trust," – intangibles which all take time to establish.

While major financial institutions with "deep pockets" can theoretically afford to keep funding a loss-making Internet venture until it begins to generate profits, smaller entities answerable to venture capitalists or other investors do not have this luxury. They must begin to generate a return for investors within a short-term time frame before depleting the seed money (the "burn rate").

It should also be noted that since financial products are relatively generic, the differentiating factor is largely performance-related. Accordingly, the financial sector has traditionally been strongly reliant on, and a heavy investor in, information technology infrastructure in order to achieve business advantage in various sectors, including delivery, trading, reporting, processing, and control. These heavy investments also tend to act as an entry barrier, although the advent of e-finance has made it easier for new players lacking a "bricks and mortar" infrastructure to mount a challenge to established players. With the exception of brand name and image, virtually all other hurdles are quite surmountable.

Players in e-finance nevertheless have found the competitive environment difficult to navigate. Many specialized players, such as Beanz (electronic money or tokens), have discontinued operations. Though barriers to entry are lower, adapting financial services to the Web remains a complex task.

IMPLEMENTATION ISSUES

The implementation issues facing banks are often difficult and contradictory. Systems can be implemented in a variety of ways, and include a range of issues, of which the following are examples.

» *From scratch* – this approach is advantageous, as state of the art systems can be designed on a clean slate, thereby using recent technology and ensuring future evolution. The strategy is possible in cases of banks building up new systems such as in Eastern Europe. It can, however, be un-cost effective in mature banks where legacy system issues arise.

» *On top of existing systems* – this is the usual case in mature markets where legacy systems representing considerable investments are present. Implementing systems on top of existing systems requires integration skills and value-added competencies. Here the implementation issues faced by the hardware and software teams reside primarily on system integration skills. Often solutions represent either a compromise or are cumbersome, with the use of emulators and conversion processes for databases.

» *Role of consultants* – they are usually brought in to examine the client's existing IT infrastructures and to analyze their needs, and then formulate hardware and software recommendations as well as the implementation strategy. The advantage is that a vendor-independent opinion is theoretically possible; the disadvantage is that you are dealing with generalists as opposed to specialized experts.

» *After-sales support* – a "non-technical" issue but nevertheless crucial in the long run. After-sales support dovetails with vendor reliance, and a close look at the vendor's product development strategy and long-term viability should be made. After-sales support can also include factors such as the financial situation of the company, its product development strategy, its adherence to or support of industry standards, its geographical coverage, etc.

Traditionally, banking management in general and, in particular, at the business function level (head office or branch) has been dismissive or even hostile to the ongoing role of IT and IT consultants in their business. Enlightened management has, however, already realized that further deployment of IT at the branch and individual user levels is not only useful for cutting costs but it is also vital as a strategic weapon to increase value-added services, competitiveness, and customer loyalty. This difference is likely to be at the core of the competitiveness enabling company success or failure. Enlightened management will also have realized that investment in appropriate IT systems will be central to any effort to transform banks from product-driven to customer-driven organizations, in particular at the branch level.

The Global Dimension

- » Investment banking and corporate banking services;
- » electronic forums in investment banking;
- » BOLERO;
- » global custody;
- » corporate banking, including STP, clearing, and settlement;
- » SME issues (small-to-medium business);
- » retail banking, including online trading and banking;
- » e-cash and electronic purses; and
- » critical issues for e-finance.

The combining of the growth in the Internet and new technologies with the trends of economic globalization, mergers, and concentration/internationalization of the financial services industry, is leading to numerous significant developments in the arena of e-finance. E-finance is a broad field and it is impossible to describe technical developments in meaningful detail at the macro level. These developments are impacting various specialized sectors or subsets of the financial services industry. We therefore, in this chapter, look at some discrete industry sectors and see how the impact of e-technology has affected them:

» Investment banking and corporate banking services
» Electronic forums in investment banking
» BOLERO trade finance
» Global custody
» Corporate banking
» Other services: STP, clearing and settlement, SMEs
» Retail banking
» Online trading
» Online banking
» E-cash and electronic purses.

INVESTMENT BANKING AND CORPORATE BANKING SERVICES

While investment banking is still, at its core, a relationship business driven by personal contacts and face-to-face negotiations, certain aspects of the discipline are now being conducted electronically.

JP Morgan Chase has developed a dedicated Web platform for its investment banking clients known as ChaseSpace. This is basically an elaborate "brochureware" Website diffusing Chase documentation such as research, streaming audio/video reports, market commentary, securities prices, and other deal-related information. Most other major banks have also set up similar elaborate "brochureware" sites.

The development of Websites enabling actual trading, however, is another story. Much progress remains to be done in this area owing to cultural reticence and security concerns. Some developments have occurred in the secondary loan market trading area. Other key areas of online investment banking center on matching buyers and sellers of businesses or loans, and linking users and providers of private capital. We shall consider each of these cases in this chapter.

ELECTRONIC FORUMS IN INVESTMENT BANKING

Loan Syndications and Trading Association (LSTA) and Loan Market Association (LMA)

The Loan Syndications and Trading Association, Inc. or "LSTA" was established in December 1995 in the USA in an effort to develop standard settlement and operational procedures, market practices, and other mechanisms to trade the increasing volume of par and distressed bank debt more efficiently. The establishment of the LSTA inspired the formation of the Loan Market Association (LMA) in 1996 in London with the objective of fostering an environment in the euromarkets that would facilitate the constructive development of a secondary market for loans. The Association was established to bring greater clarity, efficiency, and liquidity to the relatively under-developed secondary market that existed at the time and to enable more efficient loan portfolio management.

The use of Internet and Web technologies is central to the tying together of a hitherto disparate and fragmented community into a liquid market. The LMA represents a group of bankers who are influencing the way the debt markets are conducting their business. What had traditionally been a people-driven, paper-intensive business has migrated to the Internet for sake of communications, information diffusion, and loan syndications and trading. While actual transaction processing is not within their remit, their use of the Internet has resulted in increasing trading liquidity in the market, and a forum and meeting place for bankers to co-ordinate discussions, transmission of information, and market developments. The use of the Internet and the LMA Website, which has a public front and a members-only front, is a key component of this strategy. Five initial aims were detailed at the outset:

» standardize and simplify the sale of loan assets;
» establish a market standard for settlement procedures;
» establish codes of practice for market activity;
» establish a loan valuation mechanism; and

» persuade borrowers, banks and other market participants of the merits of a more structured and liquid loan market.

This initiative was clearly well-timed as 1997 saw a rapid growth in secondary loan activity in the euromarkets, with volumes increasing to a level estimated at over $20bn for the year, rising to $28bn in 1999.

The LMA has expanded its activities to include all aspects of the primary and secondary syndicated loan markets. It sees its mission as becoming the authoritative voice of the syndicated loan market in Europe *vis à vis* banks, borrowers, regulators, and other affected parties. The Association is organized around several committees, these being the main ones:

» Distressed Debt Committee – to help create an efficient market for distressed debt by the development of standard documentation for distressed debt trades.
» Documentation Committee – to create documentation for the primary and secondary loan markets.
» Loan Portfolio Management Committee – to make proposals addressing loan trading issues so as to promote liquidity in the secondary credit markets.
» Settlements Committee – to develop standard trading, settlement, and operational procedures for the administration and trading of loan assets in the primary and secondary market.
» Systems and Technology Committee – to remain informed of technological innovations of relevance to the syndicated loan markets and to act as a contact point for service providers.

The main achievements of the LMA are these:

» Produced standard confirmations, terms and conditions, and a variety of transfer documents for both bank debt and claims.
» Produced user guide for the above, including comparison between LMA and LSTA standards (Europe and USA).
» New documentation sent to members and posted on the Website.
» Events diary created on the Website to flag conferences and events.
» Established co-operation agreements with a number of e-trading platforms to foster use of LMA documents.
» Ongoing program of upgrades to Website.

» Weekly pricing information posted on the LMA Website from April 1999.
» Agreements concluded with major financial publishers to show the Summary Survey in magazines and on electronic information services.
» Pricing graphs for individual loans available on Website Valuation Survey.
» Percentage price change index posted on Website.
» Feeds from Standard & Poor's Ratings Services and Moody's Investors Service Ltd into Valuation Survey.
» Links to Loanware information on deals on Website Valuation Survey.

And the future aims of the LMA are as follows:

» Work with LSTA and LMA towards harmonization of documentation and market practices.
» Promote recommended forms of primary documentation.
» Raise the profile of the LMA in continental Europe and the Middle East and within member organizations.
» Improve two-way communication with members.
» Develop a closer dialogue with LSTA and LMA.
» Support entry of non-bank investors into the syndicated loan market.
» Loan portfolio management.
» Improve communication with similar groups in other major financial centers.
» Promote the use of leading edge technology to establish the concept of "straight through processing" for trade settlement systems.
» Facilitate a fair and consistent trading environment and enhance liquidity within the secondary loan market.
» Develop total return and ratings indices.
» Develop a loan pricing calculator.

An electronic forum for corporate banking

In a similar vein to the LMA, investment bank Merrill Lynch created an electronic forum to service small business mergers and acquisitions (M&A). The platform employs Web technologies and proprietary databases to match clients selling businesses with potential buyers registered through a central database. Corporate banking services have also migrated to the Web over the past few years. While retail banking pioneered the move towards electronic banking, major banks have also started to use Web technology to deliver banking services to their corporate customers.

Developing a Web marketing strategy, however, is difficult for several reasons. For example, retail client relationships can be managed at a single contact point while a corporate banking relationship can be multifaceted. Banks often have several contact points with a corporate customer, depending on the nature of the relationship and the extent of financial products provided, (e.g. FX trading, corporate lending, and raising equity). The coordination of communication between areas of the bank that compete with each other can be difficult.

In addition, addressing legacy system issues within corporate banking can be complex, as individual institutional business units often use different front and back end systems. Web-based corporate banking services are centered on several key areas, including cash management, electronic bill payment, treasury management, trade finance, leasing, credit lines, and purchasing/procurement. In treasury management, many Web platforms offer corporate customers electronic access to short-term investment and liability management services,

BOLERO

Trade finance has emerged as another logical area for electronic intervention. Trade finance is a heavily documentary and regulatory process involving letters of credit, bills of exchange, bills of lading, and other credit instruments related to the shipping, importing, exporting, and financing of goods. The manual nature of the documentary process lends itself to automation, and various international banks provide standard electronic templates for different aspects of the business. These documents, accompanied by digital signatures, can be distributed electronically to relevant trade participants, saving time and expense.

Cultural resistance met in implementing such mechanisms worldwide, however, is a daunting challenge since many countries have their own regulatory structure and are reluctant to relinquish sovereignty even in a bureaucratic sense, thus hindering the take-up of initiatives such as BOLERO. International trade has traditionally been fraught with financial, logistic, and time inefficiencies, costing world business hundreds of billions of dollars every year.

BOLERO, which stands for Bills of Lading Electronic Registry Organization, is an initiative set up by SWIFT and the TT Group to provide the electronic processing of international trade, a hitherto paper- and procedure-intensive process fraught with delays. Its aim is to reduce international trade inefficiencies by moving world trade onto the Internet, allowing documents and data to be exchanged online between all parties in the trade chain. Here are the key features of BOLERO.

» Global reach – seven out of the world's top ten banks have now signed up to bolero.net, as well as major trading houses such as Mitsui and Marubeni, and carriers such as K Line, Cosco, and Evergreen.
» Open platform – unlike "proprietary" developments that force businesses down one particular path, bolero.net is committed to providing a neutral, open system.
» Certainty – a ground-breaking, globally patented legal infrastructure creates "certainty." Every member of the bolero.net community is properly vetted and bound by its structures.
» Security – bolero.net matches and exceeds the comfort factor that businesses currently have when conducting trade transactions by paper. With a messaging system operated by SWIFT, bolero.net's services utilize the latest encryption technology, messages are validated, and a rigorous registration procedure acts as the gatekeeper for prospective members of the bolero.net community.
» Information exchange – boleroxml is a validated, global, cross-industry XML standards solution that allows all parties of a trade chain to "talk" seamlessly to each other by automating their information exchange.

In order to take advantage of improved business efficiencies and effectiveness that are associated with bolero.net implementation, customers will need to have their computer business applications interface with bolero.net. BOLERO has therefore formalized its relations with third party vendors by creating a "Partner Program." The program aims to promote "bolero.net partners" to provide software interfaces and associated customer services, including consulting, project management, systems integration, training, etc. The Software Solution Provider Agreement provides for accreditation of a software product that is intended as a user system with the BOLERO product. The Consultancy Service Partner Agreement is intended to cater to companies who are able to offer implementation or project services to users.

GLOBAL CUSTODY

Global custody has been a considerable growth area throughout the 1990s and will continue to be so during the years ahead. It is a highly attractive and profitable activity to banks that have the necessary "reach" for this type of activity. The IT spend in global custody by banks is huge, and substantial opportunities exist in IT consulting, systems integration, and solutions-providing activities. Growth rates have doubled every four years and have exhibited strong performance since the mid 1980s.

The amounts invested in IT for global custody are massive. State Street, for example, channels 20% of its total expenses on IT maintenance and improvement, and has 150 computer programmers dedicated to this task. Deutsche Bank, a minor player, is spending DM250mn annually on IT for custody alone – over 10% of the bank's total IT spending.

The market is experiencing a shakeout of marginal players. Mergers, acquisitions, and consolidations lead to problems of integrating disparate legacy systems and data feeds, and offer significant opportunities for consulting. Client pressures are leading to a need to upgrade IT infrastructure: STP, upgraded facilities to extract data for management information, and interest in secure browser-based access solutions utilizing non-proprietary interfaces. Custodians are therefore having to get to grips with the Internet and the world of e-finance.

Plans for e-finance are afoot, as noted by one custodian: "We are planning to develop a browser interface with our agents for receipt and confirmation of trade instructions and for moving funds and securities." Similarly, the largest US private pension fund (Teachers Insurers and Annuity Association – College Retirement Equities [TIAA-CREF]) has developed a Website with information available for its plan participants and general public. The site allows members to review a fund's daily valuation, forward questions to the central help desk, learn about available plan options, and manage their pensions. This site illustrates at a basic level the types of services that custodians should be providing over the Net for their clients.

What is global custody?

A global custodian holds assets such as bearer-negotiable securities for a customer and ensures that administrative matters relating to the assets are dealt with. Such matters typically include the receipt of dividends or interest, deductions for tax, notification of rights such as voting rights or conversion rights arising; and if so requested, insuring the assets against loss or dealing with certain tax returns or reclamations. The custodian will also agree to make the necessary arrangements for the receipt or delivery of assets in settlement of transfers of assets (registry services) where so instructed by the customer or manager, and to report to the customer at agreed intervals the details of assets held for the customer. While this safekeeping and settlement/administrative function is technically the core of custody, custodians regard custody as an opportunity to offer additional services such as cash and currency management, tax reclamation, assisting in stock lending and repurchase transactions, and selling particular investment products such as derivatives and foreign exchange. Global custody hence has wider marketing ramifications for banks.

Managing currency, interest rate floats, and data feeds for the custody client translates into a need for robust state-of-the-art IT systems with STP capability (see Chapter 2). Systems integration is also a must, as global custodians not only act as a central depository but also they channel their electronic transfer registry services via networks such as SWIFT for institutional investor clients.

Client demands for enhanced data feeds enabling transaction confirmation, real-time portfolio monitoring, and data extraction for management information reports are becoming pressing. Clients are also demanding browser-based interfaces to access their portfolios rather than rely on traditional stand-alone proprietary workstations. This all translates into a need to invest heavily in IT, and to tie together disparate systems, stimulating demand for a variety of services in the new e-finance arena.

Global custody is expected to continue to grow steadily and firmly over the next decade because of four key factors – demographics, economics, globalization, and competitiveness – that are relatively immune to economic cyclicality. This in turn will result in substantial IT investment.

The global custodians

Global custodians have traditionally been US-based banks, although there are several European players such as HSBC, NatWest, Royal Bank of Scotland, ABN AMRO, and Paribas. In contrast to the amount of custody assets held ($4.5trn) Chase's balance sheet pales in comparison ($366bn). Citibank, a second rank custodian, has $323bn of custody assets with a balance sheet of $310bn. Specialized custodians such as State Street, with $3.5trn of custody assets, have even smaller balance sheets ($50bn). The key word in the custody business therefore is not the bank's size but the efficiency of its custodial network.

Success factors

To succeed, a global custodian must be endowed with:

» a global banking network to ensure international transaction liquidity;
» large volumes ensuring economies of scale;
» the ability to cross-market other services in order to achieve marketing synergies; and
» the ability to commit to huge amounts of IT investment.

Also, to succeed, a global custodian must possess the following capabilities.

» To offer real-time financial information, process trading results, and deliver timely confirmations in a host of currencies, worldwide.
» To record trades electronically and constantly monitor their status.
» To provide sophisticated, accurate post-trade information and performance analytics.
» To provide compliance monitoring – a "watchdog" function. In fact, some customers are now demanding software that will actually prevent the diversion of funds into unauthorized investments.
» To provide quality custody services to reduce the risk of clerical error and "lapses of focus" on the part of traders.
» To provide an efficient, seamless data-flow, regardless of where and when the trade took place, without regard for the number of intermediaries involved.

In other words, success requires STP and the ability to integrate mission-critical systems over an inherited or acquired heterogeneous legacy system. Global custodians hence no longer provide simple record keeping, accounting or safekeeping (i.e. dumb data). They need to provide "dynamic information" that can be "sliced and diced" in myriad ways, telling investment managers and plan sponsors "what happened and why," and helping them to shape their next set of investment decisions. And increasingly, this information needs to be provided over non-proprietary avenues such as browser access over the Internet.

The value-added of custody is "migrating" forward from the "post-trade" to the "trade" and "pre-trade" environments because of client pressures and demands, set out as follows:

Pre-trade period:
» financial news and market data
» performance analytics
» portfolio management
» compliance software.

Trade period:
» order routing
» global execution for all instruments
» foreign exchange
» securities lending
» cash management
» trade management tools.

Post-trade period:
» electronic trade confirmation
» performance analytics
» portfolio fund accounting
» cash sweep with automatic investment
» tax and investment compliance
» reports, slicing and dicing financial assets in myriad ways.

Entry barriers

There are high technological costs required to be a player. At State Street for example, 20 cents of every expense dollar spent by the bank is invested in technology, and that proportion is growing. The sharply expanding number of IT professionals on State Street's payroll illustrates its transformation from a bank into an information services company. Deutsche Bank, similarly, is spending DM250mn annually on IT for custody alone – over 10% of the bank's total IT spending,

Global custodians will not disclose their annual spending on technology, but privately, officials at several banks indicate that it regularly tops $100mn, and typically falls in the $100mn to $300mn range. Most have expensive online real-time remote back-up systems, in addition.

Security remains a critical barrier in use of the Internet for moving securities and funds; other topics of concern to custodians are network bandwidth and performance. The security issue may be short-lived, as the industry moves to developing protective measures such as computer firewalls. Most custodians are hoping to nail down the security issue before developing any sort of e-finance on the Net.

Global custody clients – who are they?

Typical clients of global custodians are large institutional investors with international portfolios. Such institutional investors can include corporate or public pension funds, mutual funds, unit trusts, banks, and insurance companies managing monies (usually for short-term liquidity purposes). These institutional investors are being driven by the pension fund dynamics mentioned earlier; those, plus the need to maximize return on assets (ROA). These institutional investors hence seek custodians who can:

» offer value-added services such as tax reclamation or confirmed settlement periods of one instead of three days; and
» provide enhanced data feeds enabling improved investment management decisions.

Institutional investors are looking for the traditional selling points of competitive fees, ancillary services, and a wide-spanning international network favoring liquidity. Online data extraction for management information purposes is assuming increasing importance. Extracting data from the custodian in order to customize management reports for investment management purposes (increase ROA) and enhance risk management is seen as a must. These factors have been instrumental in the recent selection of custodians by several institutional investors.

Such services obviously require straight through processing (STP), integrating disparate systems, as well as the ability to manipulate and extract data for MIS purposes. Various surveys querying custodians about their latest systems development efforts confirm that STP figures at the top of the list. Achieving true STP capability, facilitating the settlement process that reduces risk and cost for domestic and cross-border settlements, is of key importance.

STP is absolutely essential for custodians to evolve from a fragmented collection of transaction processors to an efficient set of interconnected information processors. The old paradigm as based on standards for messages and formats is now being replaced with a new one based on standards for processes.

Information feeds

Global custody has been radically transformed by computers in the past 20 years, going from a very physical business of executing securities trades to a largely passive business of receiving and distributing feeds of data from various databases. The business has gone from being able to settle a trade in a given market – which all the major custodians can do now – to how much information can be delivered, how quickly, and in what customized format. The objective is to provide a richer content value in such information, and to use the Internet as a delivery vehicle. As global custody has shifted to an information business, institutional investors have come to rely on these service providers. The custodian is "the most important relationship I have," says one pension fund manager.

Technology is also pushing securities transactions toward STP and T+1 (next day) instead of T+3 (on the third day after the transaction) settlement. The trend is to move away from installed desktop software in favor of servers at the bank that investors can enter with basic Web browsers. There they can view an array of reports and download the files and reports they want.

Today's custodians add value in the data extraction process – by leveraging the data they control into a series of useful management reports that highlight portfolio trends, apply risk management policies, identify non-compliance problems and measure the performance of investment managers in an effort to retain/win business. Institutional investor clients, however, are starting to make demands. And while the issue of security continues to linger in regard to using the Net for serious business, it is slowly moving to the back-burner (see above "Entry barriers").

CORPORATE BANKING

Corporate banking has been a heavy user of IT. In order to provide bespoke and personalized services to major corporate clients, major banks in certain cases have partnered with technology providers to create dedicated corporate banking services. For example, Citibank and Bottomline Technology have produced an online corporate billing system; and Bank One has partnered with EDS to produce a joint invoice/payment solution. Here are some examples of facilities offered by individual banks.

» Citibank offers its corporate customers billing, cash management, custody, and trade finance services.
» Deutsche Bank offers cash management, portfolio management, and custody applications.
» Chase offers loan syndication, purchasing, trade finance, global custody, and treasury management services.
» Bank of America features treasury management and capital markets services.
» Royal Bank of Scotland offers payment/reconciliation, export collection, letter of credit, and cash management services.
» Svenska Handelsbanken and ABN AMRO offer treasury and trade-related services.

In 2001 a banking consortium including Banco Santander CH, Commerzbank, Royal Bank of Scotland, San Paolo IMI, and Société Générale introduced an online platform for corporate customers which allows them to deal in treasury and capital markets products (including FX, syndicated loans, and interest rate derivatives).

Other services: STP, clearing, and settlement

Though back-office services are not as high profile as investment banking or trading, they are an equally important dimension of the financial world. Many of the services required to support e-finance lend themselves, not surprisingly, to automation, including transaction processing, creating electronic confirms/documentation, reporting trade settlements/fails, preparing management control reports, computing valuations, managing collateral, and so on.

As noted elsewhere, collateral management, custody, and settlement, along with external services related to electronic clearing and settling of trades, have also become important parts of the e-finance processing sector. So too is straight through processing (see Chapter 2), a concept that is being promoted by many financial ventures and infrastructure providers. STP is designed to minimize human intervention in the trading and settlement process by creating a seamless front-to-back process. In its fullest implementation – which requires particularly robust and cohesive architecture – a trade input on the screen by a trader flows automatically through all of the front-, middle-, and back-office processes with no additional input or intervention. The advantages are not only that the transaction is processed more rapidly but also that it is less subject to human error.

The most comprehensive electronic STP modules, which are now linking directly into the Internet, feature a range of value-added capabilities. These typically include confirm generation, documentation creation and storage, accounting, cash management/cashiering, clearing and settling, compliance monitoring, regulatory reporting, financing, collateral management, margin management, new account handling, order handling, tax reporting and portfolio/risk reporting. Certain providers link an institution's processes directly to clearing entities, exchanges, execution agents, trade/order routing systems, and pricing suppliers, in order to provide as much real-time capability as possible.

SME clients

The SME (small-to-medium business) sector is also becoming an important focal point for various Web-banking service providers. Many established institutions have realized that SME Web banking represents an important, and largely untapped, segment of the industry. The small business banking market is already technologically wired (with Internet penetration that exceeds 70%) and lends itself to higher fees and larger balances than the retail market, making it a potentially attractive source of revenues. Industry research indicates that there are roughly 23 million SME accounts in the USA that can be readily migrated to the Web.

Most SME Web-banking platforms offer basic services such as cash management, treasury management, accounts receivable management, etc. Established financial institutions such as Chase, Citibank, Barclays, Deutsche Bank, HSBC, Société Géneralé, and National Australia Bank have tailored their storefront platforms to cater exclusively to small businesses. The significant issue here is that e-finance, which up until now has meant electronic services for major corporate clients, is now moving towards the SME sector

RETAIL BANKING

Retail banking activities have been significantly impacted by e-finance technology. From the beginning, when ATMs and telephone banking made the initial inroads, the market has evolved to more direct modes of contact with clients.

Online trading

Online trading has revolutionized and popularized the concept of Web-based retail financial services. Though electronic banking existed on home PCs well before the Internet became part of the mainstream, it was the development of useful, flexible, and secure online trading mechanisms that created consumer interest in Web-based financial services. Online trading has brought e-finance into the mass market and is the key factor in ensuring the customer loyalty that is necessary for most business models.

This mass enthusiasm is hardly surprising in that it has empowered individual investors to manage their investment and retirement assets more proactively. This occurs against the backdrop of concern over future state retirement schemes and the liberalization of investment rules allowing for more flexible and active participation by individuals. Many investors have taken a "do-it-yourself" approach to financial management, reducing their reliance on financial planners, advisers, and brokers, and conducting their trading activities via service providers such as Schwab and E*Trade.

Growth areas include mature, developed markets such as Sweden, Germany, France, and Switzerland. In most cases online trading in the US is still limited to the US markets, unless special arrangements or alliances are concluded with other international ventures, or individual subsidiaries are established in local markets. To offer customers international access, it becomes necessary to create separate subsidiaries to deal in those markets.

Features offered by most online trading platforms include real-time quotes, trade execution, research alerts, IPO access, portfolio tracking, stock filtering, financial planning, position updates, buying power notification, trade history, profit and loss accounting, multiple account access, and headline news. Trade execution modules typically let investors select the type of buy/sell order desired, including limit orders (executing at a specified price), market orders (executing at the prevailing price), marketable limit orders (executing at no worse than the price specified), good-till-cancelled orders (keeping an order "alive" until it is executed or cancelled), fill-or-kill orders (filling the entire order or none at all), and so on.

Day trading, in which investors execute dozens, or hundreds, of trades in the hope of capturing small spreads, has been in existence since the early 1980s. Most "professional" day traders, who typically trade in 500–1000 share blocks, have historically relied on electronic direct access trading (EDAT) platforms that include dedicated communications lines, guaranteed instant access to a marketplace and rich, real-time quotes. Certain dedicated retail bond trading services have also emerged, including ventures such as Bonds online, Bondtrac, BondExchange, and BondExpress. With more than 100 online trading firms in operation in the US, and a similar number active abroad, competition is considerable. As the industry matures, shakeouts, disappearances, and realignments will most likely occur.

Online banking

Online banking is a broad sector that covers checking/savings/deposits, balance information, fund transfers, payments, and credit services. Various models are used to deliver online banking services to the public. With growing demand for such services, new and established institutions have been developing their online offerings in order to meet customer expectations. Solutions providers have also striven to upgrade IT infrastructure to cater to the expected need for online banking. Some e-finance models are:

» corporate storefront model (where individual financial institutions provide clients with proprietary banking products/services);
» vertical portal model (where vertical portals operated by banks or non-banks provide customers with banking services in parallel with other services); and
» certain segments of online banking, including mortgages and loans, also making use of the marketplace model.

Though many major banks now feature sophisticated transaction-enabled services, most have had to revamp their platforms as their business model changes. Moreover, certain cultural characteristics persist – some certain industry studies suggest that purchasers of long-term deposits often like to conduct their business in person, rather than over the Web; the same is true for customers taking on large financial commitments, such as mortgages and home equity loans. It will take time before these consumers gain greater confidence with the Internet.

While total revenues derived from online operations remain relatively small at present, they are expected to increase over time as more business is conducted via the Web. It is expected that this will be the case simply due to the economic facts of lowered transaction costs once the fixed costs relating to the creation of the infrastructure are covered. Various industry studies confirm that this growth will be strong in the USA: Jupiter estimates that 25 million accounts will be operational in 2003, while IDC forecasts some 40 million accounts. The main US banks such as Bank of America, Citibank, Bank One, and Chase have made considerable progress; by 2000 the Web platforms of Citibank and Bank of America had between 500,000 and 2 million accounts each.

Online banking is also growing in Europe, Canada, and Australia. In contrast to the US however, there are very few "pure play" banks; most are ventures set up by established banks who perceive this development as a threat, and therefore feel the need to be "present." Various industry studies also confirm that expected growth in Europe will be strong, with the main markets being the UK, Germany, France,

Switzerland, Benelux, and Scandinavia. Some of these online banks carry the parent organization's brand whilst others are new brands.

Electronic payments are an increasingly important area of focus for banks. The Internet has made it theoretically possible for households to extend similar functionality to manage the electronic payment of bills and the electronic transfer of small value payments.

E-CASH AND ELECTRONIC PURSES

There are several new forms of "electronic money" in the market-place. This is known under various names such as digital currency, digital wallets, electronic money, electronic purses, etc.

Digital currency – a form of e-cash which is created through special software and which can only be used/accepted on the Web – has increased in popularity over the past few years but is experiencing difficulties as some providers such as Flooz go out of business. Digital wallets are also becoming more widely used in the B2C payment sector. These services store basic data on an embedded microchip and the card can be used either to store digital money or to contain a security mechanism to authorize transactions upon the entry of a personal identification number.

CRITICAL ISSUES FOR E-FINANCE

Computer security

Today's security issue is particularly troublesome because of the vastness of the Internet, the ease of access, and the lack of central control. Security is expected to improve as chip cards provide a protected mechanism for electronic funds. Additional developments in encryption technology, firewall systems, and surveillance systems will further protect Internet transactions. The security issue, although extremely important, is not the only or the biggest issue to address when considering the Internet for commercial use.

Global internet usage/availability

The US is technologically advanced and competitive in terms of networks. Outside the US the technology infrastructure to support the Internet is not universally in place. Some countries have limited access to the Internet (China, a number of countries in Africa, and Russia). Other countries have access to the Internet but the cost and efficiency of the ISPs and local PTTs greatly limit wide acceptance of the Internet. In the UK, user costs are exorbitantly high because of ISP charges, long distance telephone calls, and value-added tax. Other European countries have various communications improvements underway but have yet to reach the state of the US infrastructure.

The State of the Art

» New trends and business models;
» future of the e-finance revolution;
» technology characteristics;
» technology architecture; and
» issues impacting IT delivery.

EVOLVING TECHNOLOGY OF E-FINANCE

To compete in the digital economy, technology architecture has to be flexible, scalable, reliable, and cost-effective. You have to be able to change quickly to meet the demands of the market. In the financial industry, wireless technology provides a level of convenience to extend to the individual. Having a wireless extension into the technology backbone is going to be as important as having an Internet component was three years ago.

Sometimes change is happening so fast that it can be almost overwhelming. To gain some perspective we need to step back and remember how far we've come in just a few years.

NEW TRENDS AND BUSINESS MODELS

Several trends and business models are having a profound effect on the financial industry. The growing power and cost-effectiveness of communications and computing technologies, including the Internet, are at the heart of these changes. Since 1980, there have been three major paradigm shifts.

» Firstly, the transition from the mainframe to the PC, which brought computing power to the individual.
» Next, the introduction of the graphical user interface along with lower priced PCs, which made PCs easy to use, affordable and accessible to consumers.
» And thirdly, the commercialization of the Internet, which connected all these computing devices to a network.

Today, networks are outpacing the importance of the PC. The open nature of the Internet and its commercialization are keys to a revolution in the way we communicate. It has allowed one-to-one communications in ways that were previously impossible between two people, directly between business and customer, directly between business and business. Time and geography barriers have disappeared and new markets never before accessible have opened.

However, Internet technology is still in its infancy and considerable improvements in reliability and confidentiality will need to be achieved before it becomes the natural medium for e-finance.

FUTURE OF THE E-FINANCE REVOLUTION

It is of course difficult to predict the future. One thing, however, is certain – the Internet is in its infancy. We don't even know what the future e-finance landscape will be like but the use of wireless technology will no doubt feature at the forefront. Wireless technology promises to be at the apex of the thrust of new e-finance models. In fact, we may well be limited only by our ability to imagine what's possible.

For example, people will be able to use their PDAs (personal digital assistants) to buy and sell stocks whenever convenient. Customers will be able to manage their accounts, pay their bills, and take advantage of a wide range of services, using web-enabled PDAs and cell phones 24 hours a day, 365 days a year.

Microelectronics and wireless technologies are setting the stage for this revolution, and the PC will be supplemented by small hand-held wireless communications devices such as mobile phones and PDAs. Evolution of e-finance will be extremely rapid as the technology and organization strives to keep pace with demands and plans in the industry. The migration towards wireless data applications and online banking will occur rapidly – IDC predicts that more than 32 million households in the US will be banking online by 2003. Likewise, in Europe, Datamation says that as many as 21 million customers will be banking online by 2004. Change is coming faster and faster to this industry and to every household. This new wireless world will have significant impact on the financial industry in three ways.

» Firstly, wireless technology will impact business trends and new business models that are shaping the future of e-finance.
» Secondly, these emerging technologies will in turn foster even more change.
» Thirdly, the technology architecture needed to support any new business model adopted will be impacted.

TECHNOLOGY CHARACTERISTICS

A major challenge facing financial institutions is the need to react quickly to changes in the market. A formidable barrier to reacting quickly is a lack of flexibility in IT architecture. Each business model has different technology characteristics and needs. The full service provider has different technology requirements from the specialist. But the architectures for both must be flexible, yet robust, since the business models are continuously adapting to the changing needs of the market.

Distributor and portal models, on the other hand, can more easily leverage best-of-breed and the most cost-effective services available from their partners or specialized suppliers, thus allowing them to offer more easily a much broader range of services directly to the customers' desktops, or to their hands with a PDA or cell phone. If financial institutions don't have the technological flexibility to adapt it will be hard to aggregate, compete or survive in a world changing as quickly as ours. Their ability to do this will depend on the flexibility, scalability, and robustness of their technology.

TECHNOLOGY ARCHITECTURE

The key to being able to take advantage of all these new technologies and business models is a flexible technical architecture that allows companies to move quickly. There are four major components of this.

» Client access – anytime, from anywhere, using any method, to any service.
» Business applications – the applications that interface with the clients and support the products and services.
» Electronic commerce architecture – which takes care of messaging, file transfer, back-office transaction processing, settlement, CRM, and security.
» Data sources that are used by all these systems.

The global financial markets business model most likely to become the delivery mechanism for services will include:

» access by wireless, web-browsers or other thin client technology;
» access to the network via traditional telecom methods as well as TCP/IP via the Internet, intranet or extranet;
» Web services – Web-hosting FTP, bit streaming, multimedia, newsgroups, and other services;

» an interface engine that enables the ability to talk to back-end legacy systems and dynamically create Web page responses, single user identification, and password security; and

» an electronic commerce engine to reformat transactions, editing, preprocessing, routing, storing, and forwarding.

ISSUES IMPACTING IT DELIVERY

There are several issues impacting information technology delivery.

» *Global straight through processing and continuous link settlement* services will have a major impact on the technical architecture of the applications systems and the back-office. They require a robust and seamless architecture built with automated audit functions and risk controls that can perform checks and balances in real time.

» *Global labor arbitrage* allows companies to take advantage of productivity and lower labor costs around the world to reduce operational costs. So the architecture must be modular to support connectivity and access to work groups around the world via the Internet.

» *Portals* are changing the competitive playing field by reducing the cost of entry for new companies and by offering a single site where customers can browse products and services from a myriad of companies, and pick and choose the needed products and services. The technology must support real-time interconnectivity among all member enterprises for portals to work.

» *Information technology* advances now enable major financial institutions to share IT infrastructures and back-office operations to lower their unit transaction costs as well as buy their back-office services as and when they need them.

» *Biometrics* will bring unprecedented security to financial transactions. It will provide a precise way to identify customers by fingerprinting, face identification, voice recognition, etc.

» *Speech recognition* not only offers security but also new ways to accomplish old tasks easily and more quickly. Speech recognition-driven menus could offer more services than keypads offer today, making services available to customers without touch-tone phones.

» *Mass access devices* – like the PDA, cellular phones and pagers – will provide an avenue to e-financial transactions for a far wider audience than traditional PCs. Analysts say that in time, cell phones will merge with other larger-screened handheld devices, which will open the door to video and other more visual Internet capabilities.

» *Electronic wallets* and smart cards will offer yet another way for consumers to access financial accounts.

» *Internet telephony* is another new technology surging in the industry. Internet telephony accounted for 1% of global telecom traffic in 1999 and is expected to surge to 17% by 2003 and more than 30% by 2005. This development is changing the attitude of the world's established telecom players, who used to keep the same equipment for 30 years and are now being forced by Internet competition to replace equipment every two years. The use of Internet telephony will ultimately shrink the planet to the cost of a local trunk call.

These developments all point to the importance of technology architecture. It must not only support enormous growth but also be able to take advantage of new developments to accelerate e-finance and business objectives. Technology architecture can have a considerable impact on the success or failure of the enterprise.

In Practice

Four contrasting examples of electronic IT at work.

The following three case studies, from the files of international IT consultancy Computer Sciences Corporation (CSC) (see Chapter 9), illustrate the salient characteristics of successfully addressing implementation issues in the e-finance sector; respectively:

» marketing and database management tools for life insurance;
» integrated software and organizational systems for pension fund management; and
» employee benefits management and product development systems.

The salient characteristics in each of these case studies is that organizational processes and product development are enhanced and empowered via the introduction of IT products that tie together hitherto disparate elements into an integrated synergistic whole. E-finance becomes the lever by which more efficient product development and marketing can occur, and by which regulatory requirements can be met and reporting requirements satisfied.

ABBEY LIFE – FINANCIAL SERVICES IN THE UK

The Abbey Life case study illustrates how e-finance is bringing together traditional and hitherto disparate disciplines into new and powerful tools to increase the efficiency of such traditional disciplines as marketing, product research, and design. Whilst these meldings were theoretically possible, the e-finance element offers the practical integration and implementation of data processing capability to enable the company to improve its marketing efficiency as well as data processing and analytical competence.

Abbey Life, a life insurance company based in the UK, set out to improve the range of products it offered via a program named PRISM (an acronym for the services it provides – protection, retirement, investment, savings, and mortgages). PRISM was designed to raise the quality of customer service as well as increase the effectiveness of the sales process and the efficiency of head office administration. With these goals in view, CSC worked with Abbey Life from initial planning and product evaluations through to system design and development, project management, and support for PRISM's implementation – completed in August 1997.

Previously, with Abbey Life's "first generation" mobile system, sales associates gathered information on customers and processed paperwork and processes traditionally, with each process residing in "isolation." After implementation of PRISM, they are now able to carry out customer interviews using a laptop-based computer system, and effect customized customer diagnostics and proposals using the most current local customer information uploaded from Abbey Life's central computers. PRISM uses a built-in electronic template and questionnaire to enable the analysis of client requirements.

The system enables the salesman to show hypothetical scenarios of the client's options immediately on the laptop's color screen. Such scenarios could include, for example, bar charts comparing future financial requirements at retirement age with future sources of income. The graph accordingly illustrates the anticipated shortfall between the two trends, and shows how different financial products could help satisfy this shortfall in the pension target.

This sort of system is a powerful electronic improvement on typical paper-based hard-sell approaches because it enables the client to see immediately in interactive form the result of investment decisions and options. It is moreover a best of breed solution because the information processed is based upon a complete template prompting the total input of relevant client data and the processing of up-to-date information which is downloaded from the company's centralized database every time the laptop is logged into the company's network. Customers also benefit from time-saving, with a single data entry session rather than duplicate form filling, and quotations or applications tailored to their personal situation and printed out on the spot.

A key advantage to the marketing-oriented company, however, is that all customer information that has been inputted into the sales teams' laptops is automatically downloaded from the laptops and stored in a central database. This is a powerful, confidential facility that contains not only personal financial details, but also holds people's desires. It is an invaluable marketing as well as market research tool, enabling Abbey Life to "slice and dice" information in various ways, making it possible for the company to analyze trends and market requirements, develop future products, and generate leads to support the sales force.

PRISM is hence the core tool to empower Abbey Life's marketing effectiveness, and the fruit of a collaborative effort between CSC and Abbey Life to analyze, redesign, and dovetail existing sales and marketing processes, introduce the laptop system to the sales force, and structure the central customer database. The Abbey Life team brought together people who deal with customers in such areas as compliance, head office processes, marketing, and sales.

It can be seen that an e-finance project such as PRISM includes matters of product design and specification, organizational structure, e-finance, database management, and data transfer. The hybrid development and bringing together of traditional marketing disciplines with database design and management skills, bespoke software development, and communications technology effectively illustrate the melding of hitherto traditional disciplines into the new disciplines of e-finance.

Abbey Life notes that: "The implementation was remarkably smooth and hit our targets ... we would have expected more challenges to arise because this was a 'big bang' implementation; it could not be split, so the whole thing had to start at once. We are very pleased with the way PRISM is working for us, and CSC's capability was an important factor in the introduction.

"We have seen an improvement in productivity across the range of products, together with tangible time savings for the sales force and head office staff. PRISM introduced a number of features unique in the marketplace. Above all it enables us to provide a level of customer service and comprehensive information that would simply not be possible without it."

PENSION REFORM IN POLAND

Computer Sciences Corporation and International Nederland Groep (ING) of the Netherlands have worked together to establish an operating company in Poland so that Polish citizens can invest funds under the new Polish pension reform.

Background

Poland is no exception to the international trend to move away from guaranteed state pensions to more volatile privatized pensions. Concomitant with this move towards private pensions is the use of technology to enable companies to avail themselves of a competitive advantage in being able to design, process, and sell these private pension plans. The Polish government moved part of its pension fund management into the private sector on April 1,1999. While employees' take-home pay and the cost of employment to employers remain unchanged at present, the change opens the way for fundamental reforms.

Under the old system, employers paid all social security contributions into a state fund. Under the new system the employee's gross salary is increased, but it also requires each individual to participate directly in his future by paying part of the total social security contribution. Another important feature of the new pension system is that it is divided into "Pillars."

» Pillar I, the basic level to which all employees contribute, is now linked to contributions paid on behalf of individuals (employer contributions).
» Pillar II relates to employee contributions:
   » those under 30 must contribute a percentage of their new gross salary to Pillar II – a private commercial pension fund of their choice;
   » those aged between 30 and 50 can opt for the two-tier scheme or pay solely into the reformed Pillar I state scheme; and
   » those over 50 have no change in their state pension provision.

The new scheme is expected to have significant impact on the stock and bond markets – with contributions forecast at 5bn zloty (around €1200mn) to be invested in the first year and 10bn (around €2400mn) in the second year.

Pillar III is currently under consideration and aims to encourage companies to set up pension funds to incentivize employees via recruiting and retaining staff, providing additional benefits to employees over 50, and providing higher-paid staff with a loophole around Pillar II limitations. Pillar II maximum contributions are capped at a level of 2.5 times average salary.

PTE N-N

ING is bullish about the potential of the Polish private pension fund market, and aims to be present in this market via the establishment of

Powszechne Towarzystwo Emerytaine Nationale-Nederlanden Polska S.A.(PTE N-N). This company was established in 1998 by ING Continental Europe Holdings B.V. (holding 80%), and Bank Slaski S.A. of Katowice, Poland (20%), a majority-owned subsidiary of ING.

PTE N-N was licensed on October 27, 1998, as one of the first six pension funds in Poland. The company offers long-term savings accounts aimed at accumulating capital to be paid out at retirement. PTE N-N sells its product through a network of 4500 insurance advisers of Nationale-Nederlanden Poland S.A. and more than 220 branches of Bank Slaski.

Solution

ING, a global financial services provider with an established presence in Poland through its life assurance subsidiary, established PTE N-N as a special purpose vehicle designed specifically for the new pensions regime in Poland. CSC and ING together developed and implemented CSC's LIFE/400 solution, with specific adaptations for the Polish market. LIFE/400 is the technology framework that enables PTE N-N to accept pension contributions and invest and manage them according to the new regulatory regime.

CSC sales literature describes LIFE/400's functionality as follows.

» The "new business" proposal facilities allow users to enter and maintain details of each proposal received. Data is validated to ensure product rules are satisfied and once all of the data has been entered the contract can be issued. A "fast track" contract creation facility is available that enables the ability to create and issue a contract in one go. The ability to alter or cancel contracts from inception is also provided for any amendments or "cooling off" type cancellations.

» Regular processing drives the routine events that occur on contracts, such as premium billing, due date accounting (if applicable), premium collection, overdue premium notices, and anniversary processing. A number of additional user-maintainable batch schedules are provided with the base system.

» Group billing provides the ability to attach a number of individual contracts to a group entity for the purposes of premium billing, collection, and reconciliation. Maintenance facilities are also available for group-billed contracts.

» The "contract servicing" options cover the types of changes typically allowed on contracts, such as adding new or changing existing benefits, fund switches, changing premium payment details, and so on. Practically all data captured can be modified over the life cycle of a contract.

» Claims processing supports death claims, full and partial surrenders, paid up (reduced sum assured), lapse, regular withdrawals, regular benefit claims, annuity payments, and maturity or expiry processing. The paid up and lapse options can be performed online or automatically as part of the overdue premium processing rules.

» Agent management stores details of the distribution channels and intermediaries which are used to determine the commission calculation and payment rules for each agent. The open architecture caters for practically all forms of sales intermediaries. Agency hierarchies can be created with the option of generating overriding commission. The ability exists to transfer an individual contract or a portfolio from one agent to another.

» Automatic outward reassurance is supported on either a treaty or facultative basis. Treaties can be defined as surplus or quota share, and reassurance premiums can be calculated on a premium or original term basis. The reassurance for a client can be reviewed at regular intervals.

» Statistical information is stored and can be used for statutory and agency reporting purposes.

PTE N-N is already using LIFE/400 to process applications from thousands of employees who have chosen it to invest their Pillar II contributions. The short timescale, 19 weeks from start to finish, was a major challenge for successful implementation of the program.

HOLLARD LIFE ASSURANCE – JOINT VENTURE IN SOUTH AFRICA

Hollard Life Assurance Company, based in South Africa, sought to shake up the existing employee benefits market by providing a better service and information for clients, using IT to enable the creation of more flexible products tailored to suit clients' needs with guarantees in service and price.

CSC and Hollard Life together developed a new joint venture organization that provides Hollard with streamlined administration and electronic trading, focused on the employee benefits arena. Employee benefits are typically group arrangements offered by employers to employees or members and their families, for the provision of retirement funding and other security needs or benefits.

Benefits at a glance

With South Africa now integrating into the world economy, its government is looking to the private sector to participate in the provision of services to its citizens and providing for the sick and elderly. In a country with minimal social security benefits, insurance is vitally important. Hollard Life Assurance Company Limited – part of the Hollard Insurance Group – is a major South African insurer based in Johannesburg. The group employs more than 700 people and has an annual premium income in the region of R1bn. The market is witnessing increased competition, changing legislation, independent service providers, and higher expectations from clients.

Hollard Life created a division, designated "HUB," in order to position itself in the new opportunities, realizing that its existing life cover and retirement provision did not fully address the real needs of the members with the changing lifestyles and economic situation in South Africa. Products lacked flexibility, and were often a poor match for customers' needs.

HUB set out to develop "flexible products" with "multiple risk and investment choices" that would enable it to design products that could flex with the clients' changing needs. HUB accordingly realized that it would need a partner that could tie together IT capability with business experience, and therefore selected CSC because of its experience in IT and partnering with companies across the world.

CSC and HUB therefore created CSC Administration Service (Pty) Limited – a partnership administration services company in South Africa. The company was set up to build a fully integrated solution to administer all of HUB's group benefits business, and also to sell its administrative services to other players in the industry. A key element in the Hollard strategy is the opportunity for "worksite marketing."

Creating a "value-net"

At the heart of HUB's strategy was the aim of creating a "value-net" that focuses on managing relationships with clients and business partners rather than introducing products. Value-net in the Hollard vision is "an integrated environment that brings together the best competencies to deliver the ultimate level of service and product to clients." In plain English, this means that product development and marketing needs to be more client-centric. In other words, meaning that the client can make choices and that products are targeted to existing market realities and requirements rather than offering a fixed range of "take it or leave it" products.

The relationship with CSC aims to leverage on the company's experience in providing "customizeable" products underpinned by an IT structure to manage them industrially. IT, in other words, provides products with the appearance of tailor-made services but manages them as a homogeneous generic commodity. This trend is a reaction to the market's increasing sophistication and reluctance to be corralled into the straightjacket of unidimensional, fixed, "take it or leave it" products. Customization is an indispensable feature of today's more sophisticated approach to the end-user client, and is becoming a marketing imperative.

For *aficionados* of marketing-speak, this could be seen as: "There is clear evidence that a client-centric structure, offering outstanding service, quality and total reliability, is the formula for success in the future."

The right tools

The administration system is based on GraphTalk A.I.A. – a new generation software solution for the insurance industry. GraphTalk AIA is based on object-oriented technology, which means that new products can be developed and "bolted on" to the overall IT structure without necessitating changes to that structure. Whole sections or "objects" can be removed, redeveloped or reused in different products, and products can be tailored precisely to clients' needs quickly and cost-effectively. This structure obviously favors the development of "new" and "bespoke" products, thereby endowing the company with an ability to react quickly and with a competitive edge.

The solution provides a clear view of HUB's fees and costs, and how pension funds are managed. The system also offers new "freedom of choice" for clients: instead of being obliged to keep both investments and administration with the same company, they can now move investments elsewhere if they wish.

Since its launch in 1993, GraphTalk A.I.A has been licensed to some 55 insurance companies throughout the world – more than 40 of them in Europe.

Online to the future

South African banking systems are very sophisticated, and the solution is designed to use them for maximum advantage. To ensure timely payments and receipt of monies, electronic transfer of money is fully integrated with the administration and accounting systems.

The new system enables HUB to meet higher levels of guaranteed service. By obtaining clean and useful data at the client level, it enables HUB to deliver improved "guaranteed service levels." This should motivate the client to ensure that continual support is given in supplying correct information at all times. The goal is to move towards a totally IT-literate supply chain.

Implementation

The solution was designed, developed, and implemented by the joint CSC/HUB team on an astonishingly tight timescale. The project began in Paris in May 1998, when a multi-national development team got down to work, comprising four or five CSC specialists from France and the UK, and a similar number from HUB in South Africa.

By August, the new administration company was ready with fully-fitted facilities and a new IT infrastructure for the development team to work with. The team arrived in Johannesburg in September, and went live with 14 funds in November as a pilot – moving to full operation in March 1999. What was expected to be a three-year project was achieved in 18 months with the HUB/CSD partnership on the project.

HUB in effect leveraged on the accumulated IT and industry experience of CSC. While the company is known to the outside world as HUB, the group benefits division of Hollard Life, the mechanics of the venture operate with two brands: HUB and CSC.

Selling the service

South Africa's insurance industry is more prevalent than in many countries, particularly in employee benefits, because there is virtually no state social security system in place – a heritage of the country's apartheid system. The support system in place is therefore one largely developed by the corporate sector for the corporate sector. However, administration is the weak point in many of these structures; instead of advising, staff are tied up processing paperwork and analyzing claims. With this in mind, and with tougher, closer monitoring of these activities by the Financial Services Board, IT infrastructures enabling these businesses to be run in compliance with local regulatory and reporting requirements and avoiding regulatory transgressions will prove to be a worthwhile investment to ensure profitably run companies.

MONEY CROSSING BORDERS – AN INDUSTRY INITIATIVE

There are now many such examples of electronic technology having been introduced by individual financial services providers into their systems, either wholly or partly. In contrast, now follows a look at one of the banking industry's contributions to solving an increasingly pressing problem – cross-border financial transactions.

The issues of continuous linked settlement (CLS) and straight through processing (STP) have already been touched upon in Chapter 2. CLS as a concept of the G20 banking group originated in 1995 and became incorporated in the UK in 1997. But by 2001 it had become apparent that the company was losing direction; and when Joseph de Feo was appointed CEO of CLS Services Ltd in June, his remit was clear: get the project back on the rails. In the short space of time that has since elapsed, there has been a raft of senior managerial appointments in an effort to bolster the company's expertise, and the plans for the next stages of the project have been finalized (see IBS Publishing Website listed in Chapter 9). Can de Feo now deliver, and what will the consequences of failure be for the financial services industry?

It must be said that de Feo looks totally at home in the CLS Services HQ in London's docklands. His was a high profile appointment to a high profile job. He is well known in the industry from his times at Morgan Grenfell and Barclays (he was director of systems and operations at both), then as president and CEO of the Open Group. In fact, to a degree, de Feo is rejoining a project with which he was initially involved at its instigation. At Barclays he was a member of the GSTPA (see Chapter 2): the industry group at the leading edge of initiatives dedicated to facilitating cross-border transactions. It is a practical example of the cooperation necessary among professionals when setting up systems having industry-wide impact, particularly in the fast-developing technology environment of today.

Organization of the GSTPA

The Global Straight Through Processing Association is an industry group open to all investment managers, broker/dealers, and global custodians involved in the processing of cross-border trades. The Association is organized as a "Company Limited by Guarantee" in the UK, with liability limited to one pound sterling. Its Web link is listed in Chapter 9.

Objectives

The current cross-border trade-processing environment is characterized by manual procedures, multiple service providers, incompatible databases, lack of standardization, relatively high error rates, excessive costs, and a relatively high rate of expensive trade failures. The impact of each of these characteristics is exacerbated by global economic, demographic, and financial trends such as the increase in cross-border investing, an increase in the complexity of cross-border strategies, public pension reform, and the aging of the world population.

To enable industry participants to contend with the convergence of these forces, the GSTPA solution is to change the dynamics of the information flows associated with cross-border transactions. Primary objectives of the GSTPA are therefore to accelerate the flow of cross-border trades information; to reduce the number of failed cross-border trades; and to reduce the risks and the costs of cross-border trade settlements. The unique feature of the GSTPA approach to these problems is the design of a solution around the notion of multilateral interconnectivity among participants involved in post-trade, pre-settlement securities processing. In this manner the GSTPA utility will provide substantial benefits to its three types of members.

Benefits

» *Investment managers* will benefit from quicker, and therefore less risky, settlement, as well as less involvement in the settlement process. In particular, investment managers will no longer have to act as a conduit for the flow of settlement information between the broker/dealer and the global custodian. They will be able to interoperate with all broker/dealers and all global custodians through one single input (an allocation) and through one single (virtual) channel.

» *Broker/dealers* will benefit from a quicker and more efficient settlement. This increased efficiency will translate into reduced risks, both through the shortening of settlement cycles and the reduction of fails. This will result in a better use of capital and reduced operating expenses.

» *Global custodians* will benefit from more timely notification of trade information that will ultimately lead to a reduction in costs and an improved quality of operations. In particular, by providing a single, automated channel between the investment manager, the broker/dealer, and the global custodian, the GSTPA utility will reduce the expensive trade capture and repair processes that global custodians need to develop and maintain to support myriad communication processes between themselves and investment managers. Additional benefits to the global custodian include economies of scale, earlier receipt of information, and reduced fail administration and processing costs.

Key Concepts

A glossary of terms and abbreviations.

GLOSSARY

10-Q – A summary quarterly financial report filed with the Securities & Exchange Commission (SEC). All companies listed in the US are required to file such reports.

1O-K – A company's annual financial report filed with the SEC. All companies listed in the US are required to file such reports.

After-hours trading – Trading which occurs prior to, or after, the official New York trading hours of 9. 30am and 4pm; a growing amount of activity is occurring after hours through Electronic Communications Networks (ECNs) and other Alternative Trading Systems (ATSs).

Aggregator – A program that compiles financial information from disparate sources.

API – Application program interface: a software layer that connects Internet processes and platforms with proprietary or third party "front end" graphical user interfaces (GUIs).

ATS – Alternative trading system: any alternate forum for trading securities that brings together buyers and sellers.

B2B – Business-to-business: Internet platforms created by institutions to serve other institutions or alliances.

B2C – Business-to-consumer: Internet platforms created by institutions to serve individual consumers, e.g. integrated portals or Websites.

Bandwidth – Amount of information that can be sent through an Internet connection, in kilobits, megabits, or gigabits per second.

Beta development – A test version of software or technology that is functional, but still in the testing stage and not commercially distributed.

Bottom fishing – An investment strategy focusing on securities that appear undervalued compared with historical or comparative measures.

Broadband – High bandwidth, high-speed communication links that feature "always on" connections with no dial-up required, (e.g. T1, cable, satellite, and wireless).

Browser – A GUI that lets network users access information, products, and services in a simple, user-friendly fashion.

Burn rate – Speed at which an Internet venture spends funds provided by venture capitalists or other investors.

CHTML – Compressed hypertext mark-up language, a mark-up language used for wireless devices.

Clearing – When a financial transaction between a buyer and seller has been properly executed.

Computers 1st generation – Computers in the 1940s and 1950s with switching through vacuum tubes.

Computers 2nd generation – Computers in the 1950s with switching based on transistors.

Computers 3rd generation – Computers in the1960s to late 1970s with switching based on transistors contained within integrated circuits (ICs). These computers were the first to feature terminals and storage on hard drives.

Computers 4th generation – Computers comprised primarily of ICs (1970s to the present).

Cookie – Information inserted into a user's hard drive upon a visit to a Website which stores an individual's user preferences, permitting customization.

Corporate storefront – A Website that exhibits an institution's offerings; transaction-enabled storefronts allow clients to purchase the company's products and services.

Day trader – A trader who executes dozens, or hundreds, of trades during a single trading session in the hope of profiting from very small moves. Day traders close out their positions at the end of the trading day.

Decimalization – The practice of quoting stocks in single 0.01 price increments (rather than the traditional 1/16, 1/8 or 1/4 increments in use up to 2000).

Digital certificates – A digital identification mechanism used in conjunction with a public key encryption system.

Digital currency – An electronic currency, created through special software, that can be used only on the Internet.

DNS – Domain name system: a framework that manages network addresses and registrations found in URLs, e.g. .com, .org, .gov, .edu, .mil, .net, .int.

DPO – Direct private offering: a direct private placement arranged on behalf of small private companies.

DSL – Digital subscriber line: a telecommunications service that turns voice and data into packets that travel at high speeds over standard copper wire; DSL is "always on" and comes in various constructs that allow users to send and receive data at different rates.

Due diligence – The process of reviewing and analyzing the financial state of a company planning to issue securities; results of due diligence are contained in offering prospectuses.

E-cash – Electronic cash: cash which can be created on, and transported through, the Internet. E-cash can be anonymous (bearer) or registered: digital money, typically in the form of downloadable "digital coins" that can be stored in an on-line bank account, on a personal computer (PC) or on a smart card. Driven by Web-based payment schemes, electronic cash is today primarily aimed at exploiting very-small-value transactions (e.g. less than $20 or $1, or even less than a penny). Worldwide, very-small-value transactions make up trillions of dollars worth of commerce annually. Making these transactions more convenient will be big business when electronic-cash technology matures.

ECN – Electronic communication network: an disintermediated exchange-like mechanism that matches buy and sell orders anonymously. ECNs do not depend on intermediates and rely instead on price and efficiency.

E-commerce – Electronic commerce: the uses of communication technologies to transmit business information and transact business. Taking an order over the telephone is a simple form of e-commerce. Commerce conducted via the Internet is also called EC, but commercial exchanges on the Internet are only one of several advanced forms of EC that use different technologies, integrated applications, and business processes to link enterprises. Business-to-business EC focuses on transactions and communication, specifically the electronic exchange of information, goods, services, and payments. Key business processes that are carried out by EC include procurement, order entry, transaction processing, payment, inventory, fulfilment, and customer support.

EDGAR – Electronic Data Gathering, Analysis, and Retrieval: a database at the SEC's Website, housing corporate filings and registration statements.

EDI – Electronic Data Interchange: an early electronic commercial communication protocol between corporations, used for supply ordering, accounting, invoicing/billing, and inventory management.

E-finance – Electronically enabled access to financial services. It is not a delivery (i.e. institution-centric) vehicle, but a vehicle of access (i.e. customer-centric).

EFT – Electronic funds transfer: a mechanism for electronically transmitting funds between two parties.

Electronic purse – Smart cards that can be used to purchase goods/services electronically. These cards can be credited with an anonymous form of electronic cash (e-cash), and can be used to purchase goods at appropriate terminals.

Encryption – A technique designed to keep data/information private or to verify identities. Data is encrypted by software and can be constructed based on symmetric (private key) or asymmetric (private/public key) principles.

Ethernet – A standard LAN connection that allows proximate computers to connect and communicate at very high speeds.

Fill or kill order – An order to execute an entire transaction as specified, or none of it.

Firewall – Hardware or software placed between two networks that forces all in/out traffic to pass through a central point for verification, authorization and virus checking. Firewalls are designed to keep intruders or hackers from penetrating into a network.

HTML – Hypertext markup language: a metalanguage that allows for development of Web pages through standard commands, tags, and codes.

http – Hypertext transfer protocol: a communications protocol used to connect servers to the Internet.

Hybrid – An Internet strategy and structure in which an established firm has traditional physical operations as well as Internet-based operations to sell its products and services.

Hyperlink – A link on a Web page that transports the user to another Web page on the Internet.

Incubators – Companies that provide start-up ventures with seed capital, administrative services, and business plan support in exchange for an equity stake. Once the incubator is ready, it can then be presented to a VC (see below) for additional financing.

Infomediary – A Website that acts as a provider of information to individual or corporate users; it can also act as an aggregator and profiler of data.

Infrastructure providers – Companies that supply B2C and B2B platforms with consulting, software, content, communications, security, and maintenance solutions.

Intelligent agents – Software programs that can be programmed to search the Internet for user-specified information, services, and products.

IPO – Initial public offering: a public flotation of a company on the stock market.

ISDN – Integrated services digital network: digital lines capable of transmitting data at speeds of up to 128 kbps.

ISP – Internet service provider: a company that provides users with access to the Internet.

Killer application – Killer app: a software or application that becomes so popularly accepted and widely used that it forms part of daily personal/business life.

LAN – Local area network: a network of two or more computers connected and communicating over a small distance, e.g. same room or building.

Last mile – The "final link" between an end-user's PC and the tail end of a common network, such as a telephone company. This final link is typically bridged via standard copper wire, resulting in a slowing of data transmission.

Legacy system – An IT system that forms part of an established institution's operating processes; legacy systems typically have to be integrated with Web-based front end platforms to deliver full client execution capabilities.

Managed fund – A customizable fund enabling an investor to construct and alter a portfolio of stocks at will, based on personal investment and tax criteria.

Market order – An order to execute at the prevailing market price.

Marketable limit order – An order to execute at no worse than a specific price.

Marketplace – A Website grouping information on various products and services, which enables customers to search and select based on defined criteria.

MIPS – Million instructions per second: a measure of the processing/computing speed of microprocessors.

Narrowband – Dial-up access, i.e. relatively slow transmission speed and capacity compared with broadband. Narrowband is the main form of Internet access for home users.

New economy – The sector of the global economy based on "new companies" (start-up ventures or extensions of established firms) whose goods and services are based on new technologies (the Internet) and new distribution channels.

OS – Operating systems providing the environment for users to interact with a computer; individual software and interaction with peripherals are managed by the operating system. There are various operating systems such as Windows NT, UNIX, Linux, OS/2, etc.

P2P payment – Peer-to-peer payment: a system that allows consumers to transfer funds over the Internet. P2P debits the sender's credit card, e-mails the recipient, and sends the funds via transfer or check to the recipient.

Packet switching – The technique of breaking down a file or message into small packets, sending them through the most efficient route on a network, and then reassembling them at the destination point.

PDA – Personal digital assistant: a small, mobile computing device.

PDF – Portable document format: a file format enabling the viewing and printing of documents over a wide range of heterogeneous computers without loss of formatting.

Scalability – The extent to which a business model can be expanded and remain operable.

XML – Extensible markup language: a metalanguage that is becoming a standard for communication on the Internet. XML is a markup and tagging language that describes Web-based content. It helps power Web searches and can assist programs and applications in exchanging information.

Resources

Some suggested connections for further study, with Web links.

EUROMONEY MAGAZINE

Euromoney is the leading publication covering developments in the financial services industry, appearing monthly. Mergers, consolidations, and other issues pertinent to the banking industry are covered, more from a practitioner than an IT viewpoint. It is useful, however, in aiding understanding of the business pressures impacting on banks, and how these affect their strategy and business focus.

The Website also provides information on a wide range of other financial media published by Euromoney plc.

Link

http://www.euromoney.com

BANKING TECHNOLOGY

This London-based publication provides regular assessment of the state of IT technology and software market in the international financial services industry. Companion publications cover specific aspects of the IT sector.

Link

http://www.bankingtech.com

INTERNATIONAL BANKING SYSTEMS

A competitor of Banking Technology, set up by an ex-BT editor, this monthly focuses on IT, including software developments and procurement patterns. It heads a list of titles covering wholesale, retail, and private bank back-office systems.

Link

http://www.ibspublishing.com

AMERICAN BANKER

Developments in US banking, from an industry practitioner point of view. Published Mondays through Fridays. Website lists companion magazines.

Link

http://www.americanbanker.com

THE BANKER

A monthly review of global industry intelligence, from the Financial Times Business stable of related publications.

Link

http://www.thebanker.com

ISI PUBLICATIONS LTD

This site lists numerous titles covering such evolving e-markets as asset management, e-commerce, Asian market funds, and market regulation.

Link

http://isipublications.com/booklist.asp

BUTTONWOOD

NY-based management consultancy strong in global custody IT technology. It offers a newsletter and a global custody yearbook.

Link

http://www.buttonwood.com

EUROPEAN BANKING TECHNOLOGY

Addressing the state of banking IT technology in Europe, this is the Website of the Frankfurt-based organizers of an industry exhibition, together with workshops and conferences.

Link

http://www.eurobanktech.com

SWIFT

Engineering developments in financial payments, SWIFT is the original Financial Services Network, and is now moving into Internet-related payment and communications systems. The Website provides ample documentation on the function of SWIFT, also newsletters and policy papers speculating on the financial services industry of the future. See Chapter 2.

Link
http://www.swift.com

GSTPA

Associated with developments in continuous linked settlement, the Global Straight Through Processing Association is an industry grouping that is spearheading the initiatives to achieve STP. Members of GSTPA are member banks and securities players who are attempting to define the user standards moving forward. The Website issues policy pronouncements and information regarding developments in this area. See Chapters 2 & 7.

Link
http://www.gstpa.org

LMA

The Loan Market Association is the UK-based body responsible for harmonizing developments in the computerized loan trading market in Europe, and attempts to define norms and guidelines. The Website illustrates the issues and concerns impacting on a key area of commercial and investment banking. See Chapter 5.

Link
http://www.loan-market-assoc.com

LSTA

The Loan Syndications and Trading Association is the US equivalent of the LMA, having been established shortly before the European body to develop computerized loan trading in the USA. See Chapter 5.

Link
http://www.loanpricing.com

FORRESTER RESEARCH

One of the leading think tanks looking at IT developments in a broad sense and ascertaining future trends. Although the Website is heavily IT- (as opposed to finance-) oriented, considerable market specialization is provided for the financial services industry. Summaries and industry reports are available.

Link

http://www.forrester.com

GARTNER GROUP

Similar to Forrester, this research and advisory consultancy is active in providing IT and marketing intelligence for regional/global opportunities.

Link

http://www.gartner.com

IDC

Another leading provider of global marketing research and data for financial services, with strong IT orientation.

Link

http://www.idc.com

COMPUTER SCIENCES CORPORATION

A worldwide consultancy offering business solutions based on the latest IT to industries and governments (see Chapter 7).

Link

http://www.csc.com

Ten Steps to Making
E-Finance Work

Key insights into what is required for success.

- » Understand your business.
- » Understand your clients.
- » Use e-finance to simplify, not embellish.
- » Adapt, adapt, and adapt.
- » Use partnership solutions creatively.
- » Satisfy security concerns.
- » Legitimize the arena!
- » Remember customer service.
- » Plan for the future.
- » Understand how e-finance will impact your new business model.

Although the e-commerce euphoria that we experienced just a year ago is tapering, it is evident that the future economy will continue to evolve in this direction if for no other reason than to obtain and maintain competitive advantage. It is therefore not surprising that the financial services industry is continuing to forge ahead into the "e" world. There are clear signs of future opportunities and challenges for financial institutions and non-bank financial institutions such as major insurance companies.

While the opportunities still exist, they will be captured only if their pursuers adhere to the lessons learned over the past few years. Despite loss of momentum, which appears to be directly correlated with the losses on technology share prices, some fundamental initiatives will continue to be critical to institutions. Companies that want to continually increase sales need to access new markets and clients, typically via new distribution channels. By "Web-enabling" their range of products and applications, companies will be positioning themselves to leverage these new distribution conduits. This aspect of e-commerce is expected to continue to expand, as it would be shortsighted to ignore the competitive advantage of investing in this area. To obtain funding and internal support for future e-commerce initiatives, they will need to present business plans based upon positive ROI forecasts within a reasonable payback period, e.g. less than two years.

However, even more important will be the ability to use these new e-platforms on a cross-industry and a cross-product range basis. In order to achieve operating synergies, it will be necessary for companies to leverage the "e" application or product across various industry segments. We therefore consider ten essential success factors for practitioners and future practitioners of e-finance. Striving to achieve a wide appeal, many of these success factors are generic and not excessively industry- or niche-specific.

1. UNDERSTAND YOUR BUSINESS

Before harnessing technology and the e-finance model, it is crucial to understand the nature of the business you are involved in and how you will harness technology to reach this market. Too many businesses have leapt into the technology arena thinking that IT could give a new spin to an old product, and done so unsuccessfully. Before embracing technology, it is important to understand the nature of the business in question and then see how e-finance technology can facilitate the provision of key services to that client base.

2. UNDERSTAND YOUR CLIENTS

Concomitant with understanding the nature of the business are the needs of your client. It is crucial to understand what category of client you are considering when formulating your organization's e-finance strategy.

To achieve success, it is increasingly important for banks to be customer-driven. In order to focus on the real needs of customers, bank managements need access to all types of current and pertinent information, updated on a real-time basis. This means that the focus is shifting from traditional accounting-based to client-based systems. These include economic and financial information as well as all aspects of customer information, such as account patterns, product mixes, costs of sales, etc. Such information enables management to adopt corrective measures and form new business strategies. For most financial institutions, to endow themselves with such systems means that they will need to reorganize existing work practices and work flows, and implement new information technology databases and tools to achieve this.

3. USE E-FINANCE TO SIMPLIFY, NOT EMBELLISH

The main tenet in implementing technology is that ultimately it simplifies your client's life. When developing an e-finance strategy, it is essential to consider carefully the client sector you are aiming at, and how the e-finance service you are proposing will simplify your client's work processes or life.

The pitfall of many e-finance initiatives quite often resides not only in the technological, but in the marketing sphere – sometimes the structure exists but it does not lead to a product which the client needs. Similarly, the structure may lead to a product, the nature of which may appeal to a client base that is uncomfortable using technology to access the product. It is therefore crucial to consider the nature of the e-finance structure, the product, and the client to ensure that the components match up together seamlessly.

4. ADAPT, ADAPT, AND ADAPT

The "e" world has definitely changed dramatically over the last several years. Many companies with good ideas have disappeared and we can expect some additional demises in the future. For financial services providers, initiatives that will be supported will need to be based upon "traditional" business models that reward profits and efficiency gains. Further, it is clear that the competitive landscape will continue to drive consolidation and new alliances. During this period of uncertainty, it is evident that change will be constant and financial service providers will need to adapt – adapt their plans, adapt their business models, and adapt them to the developments in technology and e-finance.

5. USE PARTNERSHIP SOLUTIONS CREATIVELY

Selecting appropriate partners will be crucial to ensuring success. More and more partnerships will be formed as some of the technology companies are pressured to increase sales in a declining economy and market. Some of these companies will be forced to look toward non-traditional forms of alliance to drive profits. In addition, non-public companies with future hopes of going to market will most probably focus on developing the depth and quality of their customer base, as this will be a critical evaluation factor when it is time to issue an IPO.

6. SATISFY SECURITY CONCERNS

Security concerns will mean that there will be a greater demand for "better" low-cost solutions. Factors such as increasing competition and continued consolidation will force major financial institutions to strive to improve their cost base and pass on some of the savings to companies and consumers. Without the "trusted" environment that is expected to be relatively free from fraud, "hacking", and other potential information pitfalls, it is difficult to envisage significant revolutionary change. Key to the success of e-finance will be addressing the technological challenges and communicating this effectively to the public.

7. LEGITIMIZE THE ARENA!

The Internet payments arena includes three general types of payments: B2B, B2C/C2B, and P2P. In the future, the difference between P2P and B2C payments will blur as individuals become more like vendors of services and products (e.g. sellers on auction sites such as e-Bay). Electronic commerce, information security, and information liquidity will also provide substantial revenue opportunities for the financial services industry. The focus of each is to foster secure electronic transactions. Trusted image and archive products are expected to play even more of a critical role for companies in the future. BOLERO or GSTPA, for example, require global interoperability/acceptability, and non-repudiation and legally binding protocols, as well as the ability to provide and ultimately facilitate electronic commerce.

Primary challenges continue to be similar – they relate to global legal acceptance across multiple jurisdictions, and ability to integrate electronically multiple parties that are tied into the overall process. It will be necessary to convince corporates on a major scale that it is in their best interest to adopt and support such initiatives, as they have the clout to legitimize them.

8. REMEMBER CUSTOMER SERVICE

While many of the new "e" companies have offered excellent technological and business ideas, they have been known to falter in regard to provision of good customer service. Any successful e-venturer will understand that e-finance initiatives harness technology to provide better end service to the consumer. Seeing IT as a fix to automate and lower operating costs will no longer suffice. E-finance ideally will add to the pool of services available to the client and provide so effectively.

For example, some new products give clients browser-based access into the institution's payment systems database and allow them to view all of the transactions that they processed through that institution on a real-time basis. Again, key to this application are the security protocols and firewalls that protect each customer's data.

9. PLAN FOR THE FUTURE

The best thought-out business plans will inevitably be impacted by unforeseen technological and business developments. Changes in consumer tastes and economic conditions will threaten some business plans. Ensure that your e-finance initiative satisfies a demonstrable need and that you can modify your strategy in the light of changing business and market conditions. Success inevitably requires the ability to adjust and modify an e-finance strategy.

10. UNDERSTAND HOW E-FINANCE WILL IMPACT YOUR NEW BUSINESS MODEL

E-finance will inevitably impact the business that you are operating in and designing an e-finance future for. It goes without saying that this future impact will affect the market in ways that are impossible to predict. To manage an e-finance strategy successfully over the long term, it is therefore essential to try to understand not only how e-finance will impact your business as it becomes integrated, but also to understand how it will impact and mutate the market you are active in, so that you can anticipate and implement the measures needed to correct your business plan in future.

Frequently Asked Questions (FAQs)

Q1: What is meant by "e-finance?"

A: Read Chapter 1 under "What is e-finance," and Chapter 2 for a quick definition.

Q2: Will e-finance techniques help me speed up my accounting procedures?

A: Read about straight through processing (STP) in Chapters 2 and 5.

Q3: I am an exporter concerned about settlement of my bills. How can e-finance help?

A: Read Chapter 2 under "CLS – continuous linked settlement," and Chapter 5 under "Other services" for some global aspects.

Q4: How did e-finance develop?

A: Read Chapter 3 on its evolution.

Q5: My business has good, traditional financial systems, but I would like to benefit from the speed

offered by the new electronic technology. What are the problems?

A: You have a "legacy" which involves several issues. Chapter 4 outlines the main ones.

Q6: Is e-finance a global phenomenon?

A: Chapter 5 looks at its effect, worldwide, on the principal financial services industry sectors.

Q7: What does the future hold for e-finance?

A: Wish we knew – but some pointers are given in Chapter 6.

Q8: I'm confused by all the abbreviations and technical terms. For example, what is a DNS?

A: A domain name system, like .com. There are a lot more in Chapter 8, but no list is exhaustive.

Q9: How can I keep up with developments?

A: Read some of the publications listed in Chapter 9 "Resources."

Q10: Is there a formula for succeeding with electronic finance systems?

A: Nothing magic, but ten essential factors are considered in Chapter 10.

Index

Printed and bound by CPI Group (UK) Ltd, Croydon, CR0 4YY

13/04/2025

14656458-0003